LOVE SECRETS
FOR A
LASTING RELATIONSHIP

LOVE SECRETS

FOR A
LASTING RELATIONSHIP

HAROLD H. BLOOMFIELD, M.D.

WITH POETRY BY
NATASHA JOSEFOWITZ, PH.D.

BANTAM BOOKS
New York • Toronto • London • Sydney • Auckland

Anyone with a history of mental disorder, or who is in an emotionally unstable relationship, should not do the exercises in this book without first consulting a qualified mental-health professional.

LOVE SECRETS FOR A LASTING RELATIONSHIP

A Bantam Book

PUBLISHING HISTORY
Bantam hardcover edition published October 1992
Bantam trade paperback edition/February 1994

ISBN 0-553-35120-6

Published simultaneously in the United States and Canada

Bantam Books are published by Bantam Books, a division of Ban-
tam Doubleday Dell Publishing Group, Inc. Its trademark, consist-
ing of the words "Bantam Books" and the portrayal of a rooster, is
Registered in U.S. Patent and Trademark Office and in other coun-
tries. Marca Registrada. Bantam Books, 1540 Broadway, New York,
New York 10036.

PRINTED IN THE UNITED STATES OF AMERICA

FFG   0 9 8 7 6 5 4 3 2 1

To my wife Sirah,
daughter Shazara,
mother Fridl, and
sister Nora,
the wise women
of my life who have
taught me so many
love secrets.

—HAROLD

To my parents,
children, and grandchildren,
and to Herman
with whom I am still learning
about love secrets.

—NATASHA

ACKNOWLEDGMENTS

I wish to thank my wife, Sirah Vettese, for her editorial assistance and her contributions throughout the book. Not only did she work long hours reviewing each draft, she added much love and wisdom to the manuscript.

I also wish to thank those from whom I have drawn deep inspiration, especially Maharishi Mahesh Yogi, Arnold Lazarus, Abraham Maslow, and Carl Rogers. My heartfelt appreciation to Norman Cousins, Donna Eyman, Lenny Felder, Mike and Donna Fletcher, Herman Gadon, Susie Gomez, John Gray, Trudy Green, Crystel Hammed, Robert and Phyllis Kory, Sally Krause, Norman and Lyn Lear, Peter McWilliams, Marly Meadows, Barnet Meltzer, Ali and Sybil Rubottom, Paul Sanford, Nora and Gus Stern, Gay Swenson, John Watson, Diana Von Welanetz, Ted Wentworth, and all my friends and psychotherapy clients in Del Mar, California. I wish to acknowledge my agent, Ellen Levine, my brilliant editors, Barbara Alpert and Toni Burbank, art director, Amy King, and the staff at Bantam Books for their guidance, commitment, and creative support. I also wish to thank Kathryn Conklin, Jacqueline Roberge, and Sherri Syrek for their assistance in the preparation of the manuscript.

Much appreciation and love to Shazara, Damien, and Michael for their love, understanding, and support.

Special appreciation to Natasha Josefowitz for her wit and wisdom. Natasha is a unique poet who speaks to the hearts of people of all ages.

This book has been written for anyone, single or married, who wants to know how to create and sustain a vibrant, deeply rewarding love relationship. *Love Secrets* can help you to revitalize a long-term relationship, as well as deepen the intimacy of a new romance. This book can be read on your own or shared with your love partner. Lovers sometimes like to take turns reading one or two love secrets or poems aloud. Reading together is an invitation for you and your lover to get closer; to then put down the book and talk from the heart. Below each love secret is a specific exercise to help you apply what you have learned. Love grows stronger with practice. A lasting relationship doesn't just happen; you create it.

LOVE SECRETS

Some books proliferate with advice
teaching you how to get a man
and keep him forever

Book jackets promise
that you will know
why he is the way he is
what will make him love you
and never want to leave you.

There are books
that will help you
to not fall in love
with men who hate women

This book will reveal
how to love better
and more wisely
and thus be more loved.

LOVE IS NOT ENOUGH

- ◆ We all need to love and be loved, yet finding and sustaining an intimate relationship can be one of life's greatest challenges. Love is necessary but not all it takes to have a satisfying and lasting love relationship.

- ◆ As a divorce rate of over 50 percent indicates, love fades in the face of irreconcilable differences and accumulated resentments. Love alone is not enough.

- ◆ Almost everyone secretly has fears about his or her capacity to love or find the right partner. Even when you've found the right partner, doubts about him or her being the "right one" surface on occasion.

- ◆ To create a great relationship, you must become a skillful communicator in the complex language of the heart. Most couples spend less than thirty minutes per week sharing their most intimate feelings. No wonder relationships go stale.

- ◆ Can you and your love partner freely reveal to each other who you really are and what you really want—strengths and weaknesses, hopes and fears, successes and failures?

EXERCISE

Make a list of the qualities of your ideal love partner—all the attributes you would like him or her to have.

Now review your list. Of these qualities, how many do you possess? What aspects of your capacity to love and be loved do you need to work on?

LOVE ACHE

In the morning
I ache
for a friendly voice
to talk to me

At noon
I ache
for a face across
my lonely plate

When I walk
I ache
for a hand
I can hold

When I'm sad
I ache
for a shoulder
to cry on

When I'm happy
I ache
for an arm
encircling my waist

All night
I ache
for a warm body
to press against

All day
I ache
to hear a step
other than my own

YOU MAY BE ATTRACTED TO CHARACTERISTICS IN A LOVE PARTNER YOU LATER BECOME REPELLED BY

◆ Some people tend to fall in love with someone who can't form a long-term love relationship. One of the paradoxes of love is that we may be attracted to people with characteristics we later become repelled by. Some common examples are the following:

- You choose an insecure person for a partner knowing he or she won't leave you, but later find this person so insecure that you get claustrophobic and you want to leave.

- You find yourself fascinated by someone who has a sharp tongue or incredible wit, only to resent later being a constant butt of his or her insensitive jokes and verbal attacks.

- You like someone with whom you feel comfortable, only to find that familiarity breeds contempt. You now want more challenge and stimulation.

- You find someone who seems instantly intimate and incredible in bed, but with time discover this person is terrified of genuine feelings and closeness.

- You are attracted to someone who is defiant and "challenging," only to find that this person's hostility and defiance is now directed at you.

- You are easy prey for the expert seducer and you are fascinated by his or her ability to fulfill your wildest sexual desires. Soon, however, he or she grows bored and restless and you discover your partner needs to practice these "expert seducer" skills on the next "love 'em and leave 'em" victim.

EXERCISE

How have you set yourself up for failure in love? What old habits and attitudes keep you from building a love that lasts? What must you do to change this pattern of self-sabotage?

MEETING

When I meet a new man,
the more handsome he is
the less attractive I feel
the more intelligent he is
the stupider I sound
the smoother he is
the more awkward I seem.

In other words,
when I meet a man
I really like
I become this blubbering idiot
and he will have nothing to do with me.

When I meet a man
I'm not interested in,
I am beautiful, brilliant
witty and fun
so he falls madly in love
with me
but I will have nothing to do
with him

The trick is to be dull
with the men I don't like
and sparkling with the ones I do,
but for some reason
it's always the other way around.

LOVE IS NOT A LICENSE TO SEEK TO CHANGE OR CONTROL YOUR PARTNER

♦ You may be carrying unrealistic expectations that cause significant dissatisfaction in your love relationship. If a parent or ex-spouse catered to every whim and desire, you may be expecting your love partner to live up to an impossible standard.

♦ Conflicting expectations are the source of many quarrels and much unhappiness. Which of the following common expectations cause conflict with your love partner? You must:

- like my friends and want to socialize with them
- make family priorities more important than work
- include me in all your activities
- never do anything that upsets me
- lose weight and stay in shape
- make me happy
- agree with me
- make more money
- be more affectionate and attentive
- never be attracted to anyone else
- be the first to make up when we argue

♦ Now, review the statements you have checked and consider the following: How realistic are your expectations? What is it you are looking for from your partner? What could you do to create more of what you want and impose fewer expectations on your love partner?

♦ No lover can possibly live up to unrealistic expectations or a fantasy. Love is not a license to demand the impossible or seek to change and control your love partner.

♦ Some expectations, of course, are appropriate. For example, if your lover abuses alcohol or drugs, has a history of infidelity, or is unable to make a living, you are right to set firm limits.

E X E R C I S E

A useful tool to discover more about your hidden expectations is to say, "If you truly loved me you would . . ." and then write down ten specific responses. You can lighten up these expectations, and turn them into preferences by now substituting "It would be nice if . . ."

FANTASY AT A PARTY

Too many people
I sit alone
My eye catches his
What a good-looking man
He smiles
I smile back
He comes over
A bit tentatively
And asks shyly
If he can sit next to me
"Please do," I say
He's a doctor
Or writer,
Or doing some fascinating research
And we find mutual friends
Shared interests
We like the same books
He knows about music and art
Well traveled
And independently wealthy
Single, of course
He touches my hand
Shivers run down my spine
The chemistry is right
Electricity's in the air
I am filled with happiness
And excitement
I am alive
Tingling
This is it—

Why doesn't he ever
Come to the same parties I do?

WHAT YOU RESIST, PERSISTS; WHAT YOU ACCEPT, LIGHTENS

♦ In a love relationship that isn't working, each person feels like "poor me." The more you try to change your love partner and prove how wrong he or she is, the more he or she will try to prove you wrong. The more you resist accepting your love partner as he or she is, the more his or her traits will persist in annoying you.

♦ Openness means being willing to communicate your deepest feelings. Sharing ideas, values, or convictions is relatively easy. For intimacy to grow, feelings—both positive and negative—must be shared.

♦ Self-exposure requires some risk of being hurt; courage may be called for. But in an atmosphere of acceptance, you can gradually bare the most sensitive areas of your soul.

♦ Being open and getting to know and be known by a lover is exciting and emotionally enriching. Angrily "letting it all hang out" just to make yourself feel better can be unkind and unwise. Just as important to intimacy as openness are appropriateness and good taste.

♦ There is no excuse for damaging your spouse's self-esteem with, "You are stupid and worthless." You get the picture; spontaneity must always be balanced with kindness, care, and respect. Acceptance, not contempt or arrogance, is the best basis for requesting change.

EXERCISE

What are your three biggest fears, foibles, or failings? What are your love partner's three most significant fears, foibles, or failings?

If friends and family members were willing to give you the worst possible but most honest feedback about yourself, what might they say?

When did you last cry by yourself? Why?

CONUNDRUMS

I can't allow myself to be known
unless I can trust the man I'm with
I can't trust him
unless I know him
I can't know him
until I know how he responds to me
he won't know how to respond until he knows me
but
He can't allow himself to be known
unless he can trust the woman he's with
he can't trust me
unless he knows me
he can't know me
until he knows how I respond to him
I won't know how to respond
until I know him
but
we can't allow ourselves to be known. . . .

NEVER ASSUME YOU KNOW WHAT YOUR PARTNER IS "REALLY" THINKING OR FEELING; LOVERS ARE NOT MIND READERS

♦ It is not unreasonable for you to perceive your lover's motivation or actions differently from the way your lover perceives them. It is unreasonable, and a breach of trust, for you to deny your lover's report of his or her feelings, thoughts, and experiences.

♦ Assumptions can also be used to invalidate a loved one. Statements like "You're a mama's boy" or "Don't project your hostility toward men onto me" are psychobabble. Such comments are never helpful, just thinly veiled, hostile name-calling.

♦ The solution to making assumptions is very simple. Ask your love partner how he or she feels and accept the response as true. You cannot argue with another person's feelings.

♦ Cultivate your ability to listen. Your lover wants you to understand how he or she feels, not how you think he or she ought to feel. Be receptive, without interrupting or jumping to conclusions, so your love partner feels listened to and can freely share.

♦ Love is respecting the mystery of your partner; accepting you will never understand him or her completely.

EXERCISE

Here are examples of some common but unhealthy assumptions:

- "Somewhere there is a perfect lover and a perfect relationship."
- "It is selfish and wrong to put my needs before the needs of my love partner."
- "Avoid disagreements and difficulties whenever possible; peace is worth any price."

What assumptions do you make about your love partner that would be good to check out? What assumptions do you think your love partner makes that you wish he or she would check out with you?

FALSE EXPECTATIONS

A woman marries a man
expecting that he will change
but he doesn't

A man marries a woman
expecting that she won't change
and she does

LOVE GUARANTEES SOME HURT, ANGER, AND FRUSTRATION; IT GOES WITH THE TERRITORY

◆ Love guarantees some hurt, anger, and frustration; it goes with the territory. Remember, underneath the anger is hurt and underneath the hurt is love. Caring makes one vulnerable.

◆ Keep in mind that arguments are a signal that your love partner needs care and understanding from you. Be willing to give a warm hug from your side instead of waiting for your love partner to take the first step. It may feel awkward and risky, but the rewards for being open with your positive feelings are enormous.

◆ You must also learn to accept your lover's occasional criticism. Do not resist, justify, or apologize. Simply go about your self-nurturing activities. Many people complain that their lovers always criticize them when, in fact, they criticize their lovers for criticizing them.

◆ Certain words and phrases inadvertently cause negative results. When you say to a loved one, "I love you, *but* . . ." you actually make a coercive statement that implies, "I won't love you unless you do what I say." On the other hand, if you say, "I love you, *and* I prefer if you would . . ." you communicate your love, and your feedback is more likely to be effective.

EXERCISE

Next time your love partner is upset, instead of becoming defensive and attacking, ask yourself the following questions:

- What reason does my lover have for thinking, feeling, or behaving this way?
- Why do I allow it to affect me negatively?
- What can I do to convey more love, understanding, and acceptance to my love partner right now?

BEFORE AND AFTER

During the courtship he talked a lot
of his hopes, fears, and expectations
he shared his feelings
and expressed emotions

During the courtship she listened to him
was very warm and very loving
and spent hours telling him
how wonderful he was

He was thrilled to be marrying
such a passionate woman
She was thrilled to be marrying
a man who could communicate

After the wedding
he worked very hard came home tired
read the paper
and didn't want to talk

After the wedding
she became harried
was always exhausted
watched TV
and didn't want sex

If they could
hug and talk
about not hugging
and not talking enough
they could meet
each other's needs again

LISTEN TO YOUR LOVE PARTNER'S CRITICISM WITHOUT INTERRUPTING, JUDGING, OR CONTRADICTING

♦ One of the greatest gifts you can give someone you love is to hear his or her anger without becoming defensive. One of the greatest gifts you can receive is quality feedback about your opinions and behaviors.

♦ When criticism is used in excess, both love partners are essentially saying, "I love the person I'm hoping to change you into," which implies, "I don't love you the way you are."

♦ We resent not being appreciated by those closest to us, yet we often don't see that they also need to be listened to and understood. The more you resist listening, the more your love partner will persist in giving you what you don't want to hear.

♦ Just as you would not want to disagree when someone says, "I don't like carrots," so it is pointless to try to argue with a loved one about the way he or she feels about you. Rather than shouting, "You don't know what you're talking about, it's not true," seek to understand why your partner feels that way.

EXERCISE

Next time you feel criticized by a loved one, instead of trying to justify yourself—i.e., defend yourself and convince the other person to feel differently—listen and be patient. Let go; don't try to make your love partner's perceptions or feelings wrong. Give your undivided attention without jumping to conclusions or planning your next move. You can support and encourage by using phrases such as, "I understand how you feel"; "I appreciate what you're saying"; "Tell me more."

ASK ME, DON'T TELL ME

If you ask me softly
how I am
you are just
seeking information

IF YOU TELL ME LOUDLY
HOW I AM
YOU ARE MAKING
AN ACCUSATION

TRUST

I don't know
What is best for you.
But I trust you to know that.

I know
What is best for me.
And I trust you to trust me.

NO ONE GETS 100 PERCENT APPROVAL

♦ Your love partner is sometimes going to dislike something you say or do no matter how hard you try to please him or her. Occasional disapproval is inevitable.

♦ Trying to please everyone all the time is simply impossible. No one gets 100 percent approval. Trying too hard to always please will run you ragged, and eventually cause you resentment.

♦ You and your lover may respect each other very much, yet you are going to have some opinions, traits, or behaviors that you each disapprove of. Rather than feeling hurt or angry when you face such disapproval, know that some criticism is normal in any love relationship.

♦ Learn to appreciate a loved one's different point of view. What you may have experienced as disapproval may be nothing more than your love partner expressing his or her own preferences or a different value system.

♦ Empathy means listening receptively without becoming defensive. It means striving to see a loved one's frame of reference, including how he or she views you and your actions. Place yourself in your loved one's shoes and you might feel the same way.

EXERCISE

To overcome the approval trap, distinguish between "facts" and "judgments." For example, "I work as a full-time housewife and mother" is a fact. "I am only a housewife and mother" is a judgment. Stop measuring yourself against other people's standards. Know the high worth of who you are and what you do. It is good and appropriate to be your own best cheerleader.

THE TRUTH

She loves him because
she knows him so well

She loves him in spite of
knowing him that well

LOVE SECRET #9

WHEN IT COMES TO FEELINGS, NO ONE IS WRONG

♦ Human beings can be incredibly self-righteous. In an argument, it is easy to know how right you are and how wrong the other person is. Neither side wants to give in, and both sides feel misunderstood. Each of you has a chorus of like-minded friends who unequivocally support how right you are, and how obviously wrong your love partner is.

♦ When both lovers are defending "I'm right and you're wrong" positions, a simple discussion of a specific issue can evolve into a powerful struggle of wills. You may think you are arguing the merits of an issue, but you wind up responding emotionally, as if you are fighting for the survival of your basic self-worth.

♦ Trying to "win" when you and your lover disagree is a futile endeavor. The urge to win is associated with the need to be one up and force your love partner to be one down. This competition inevitably leads to both lovers losing. Even if you "win," your lover feels defiant and upset for being turned into the "loser." You will soon pay for it in diminished affection or more quarreling.

♦ The "I'm right" syndrome can make it difficult if not impossible to accept valuable feedback from your lover. If your lover criticizes a cherished belief, you may feel so put down that you resist whatever else your lover may say.

♦ Most disagreements between lovers have to do with priorities, recollections, choices, judgments, values, opinions, and other purely subjective perspectives. Consequently, there is usually no absolute standard for measuring who wins or what is fair.

EXERCISE

The next time you find yourself in a dispute with your love partner, aim for a resolution in which you both win, both are right, and, as much as possible, both get your needs fulfilled.

When I'm Fully in Charge of Me

When I'm fully in charge of me,
    I can let you too be free.

When I am using my fullest potential,
    I can help others do the same.

When I am empowered and strong and sure,
    I feel neither envious nor threatened.

When I can grow at my own rate,
    I do not fear your taking anything away.

I do not fear your overtaking me.

SAFETY AND TRUST ARE MORE IMPORTANT THAN LOVE

♦ Heart-to-heart communication requires an emotional atmosphere of caring, safety, and trust. Even if your lover is uncooperative at first, the more self-disclosing you are, the more open and honest your love partner will be. Talk patiently from your heart and soon your love partner will join you.

♦ On some level, love partners may be afraid of each other. You may fear being hurt, rejected, or abandoned. Perhaps you're scared to reveal your small, dark, or petty side. Even lovers try to impress, suppress, guard, and conceal in order not to be found out, not to stand naked and vulnerable. Fear inhibits love.

♦ During courtship both partners are image-conscious, striving to be on their best behavior. As love matures there is less need to contrive; defenses can be dropped. Not that you get sloppy or inconsiderate, but it is freeing to learn that you don't have to be a mystery man or a glamorous woman, that you can let your hair down and still be loved.

♦ Honesty means a willingness to risk having your weaknesses and imperfections seen by your partner. You don't have to hide your scars, false teeth, or neurotic tendencies.

♦ A healthy love relationship allows two people to fully know each other and—miracle of miracles—still love each other! Being able to share yourself in an atmosphere of safety and trust is the key to overcoming the fear that inhibits love.

EXERCISE

What weaknesses or imperfections (i.e., too neat or too sloppy, too fat or too many wrinkles) would you prefer to hide from your love partner? When and how do your worst psychological foibles and neurotic tendencies show up? Be specific.

I'M NOT OK, YOU'RE NOT OK, BUT THAT'S OK

I have done bad things in my life
have had bad thoughts
I am not always kind
nor always generous
I have placed myself first
I have lied, cheated
I have acted out of passion
which has hurt others.
I have been inconsiderate
punishing, even vengeful
and I have felt guilty
tried to make amends
tried to atone
made New Year's resolutions
about becoming better.

I know some very similar things about you.
So I'm not OK
and you're not OK
but that's OK

RESPECT IS ESSENTIAL TO LOVE; NOTICING WITH ATTENTION

♦ In a healthy relationship you take joy in your partner's growth and respect his or her individuality. Many people live with a two-horned dilemma: a fear of being less or settling for less. Either way you lose.

♦ Webster's defines *respect* as "noticing with attention." The loved one is not taken for granted, but seen freshly, as if anew. Respect means more than holding your love partner in high esteem—it also means giving to him or her of your time and energy.

♦ Lovers each take pleasure in the accomplishments of the other. A wife's fame can outshine her husband's (or vice versa); there is no need for envy. There is no sense of threat, but rather pride. This is not always easy, as many men have been brought up to equate masculinity with success, and conversely, many women have been brought up to equate success with lack of femininity. This is changing, but slowly.

♦ In a neurotic relationship there is a need to put down one's partner in an attempt to build oneself up. Healthy love has no top dog or bottom dog, just two playful puppies. The other person is never coerced "for his or her own good."

♦ Disdain for another may be a sign of weakness felt within oneself. A person who has grown comfortable with himself or herself becomes more tolerant of a love partner's idiosyncrasies and weaknesses. Indeed, pet foibles can make the other person even dearer.

EXERCISE

List the behaviors or qualities that you do not respect or have difficulty accepting in your love partner. Close your eyes and try to imagine what might happen if somehow you were able to unconditionally accept these traits. How might that acceptance enhance your relationship? Whenever you start to feel disrespectful or hypercritical, stop, take a deep breath, and focus on becoming more accepting.

DEALING WITH HER SUCCESS

His wife is very successful
she earns more money than he does
has a higher position
commands more attention
has perks he does not have
sits on the board of directors
and flies in the corporate jet

He's happy for her
but he's not happy for himself
she used to be his wife
now he's just her husband

He says he doesn't mind
he even says it is wonderful
but he's not telling the truth
because he's ashamed
to be jealous
because he feels guilty
to be envious
and there is absolutely no one
he can tell this to

If he doesn't tell anyone
he'll never find out
that in our culture
most men have been raised
to feel that same way
and that it doesn't have to be like that

BLAMING AND
COMPLAINING DON'T WORK

♦ Blaming and complaining don't work. Most of us tend to blame others for the emotional upsets we have: "Stop making me feel guilty"; "After all I've done for you, this is the thanks I get"; or "It's your fault; don't come crying to me."

♦ Your lover is the most convenient person to blame for your flaws, failures, and flops. How often have you shrugged your shoulders, pouted, or complained in order to manipulate your love partner into doing something you could just as well have done for yourself? ("Where's the butter?"; "I can't find my pants.")

♦ How often have you told your love partner to make a decision for both of you and then complained about the outcome? ("Why did you pick this lousy movie?"; "This Chinese restaurant is awful.")

♦ Complaining about your love partner is an ineffective way of getting what you want. By assuming that your lover has control of your happiness and satisfaction, you will continue to be stuck in a rut. On the other hand, when you take 100 percent responsibility for what transpires between you and your love partner, enormously different results will occur.

♦ Cultivate preferences instead of demands. You might prefer Italian instead of Chinese food, and want sex tonight, but if you have Chinese food and your love partner is not in a sexual mood it doesn't matter, there is no disappointment, your love and happiness remain untouched.

♦ You can break the blaming habit by acknowledging more—catch your lover doing something right. Shifting your attention from nagging to acknowledging is a powerful relationship-changing skill.

EXERCISE

List the traits, quirks, and flaws you can't stand in your love partner. Can you look beyond these faults? Can you forgive these minor irritations and see the specialness in your love partner?

I Did It Again

I did it again.
The wrong resort.
I tried to save money,
all prepaid, of course.
It's not south enough,
the water is too cold,
the waves are too high,
the pool is too small,
the beach is crowded,
not much sun,
and I'm unhappy
dreaming of warm lagoons
where I'm not.
So
I walk around town,
sit in my room, and
read about places I'd rather be.

PROBLEMS ARE EQUALLY CREATED

♦ When problems occur, one or both love partners may take great comfort in believing the other is more to blame. One of the ways of avoiding equal responsibility is to ignore the reality that all of your choices have consequences. Whether resolution of a problem is constructive or destructive depends on you.

♦ If your intention is to prove your partner is at fault and merely to strike back, then your anger is almost inevitably destructive. You wind up trying to put down, punish, or manipulate your lover, while the positive goals of communicating needs and changing the relationship go unmet.

♦ A destructive quarrel is often a self-fulfilling prophecy in which anger begets anger. Here is what you need to watch out for to avoid destructive arguing:

- Manipulative comments to coerce your lover. ("If you loved me, you would . . ."; "If you don't like it, leave"; "Do what you want, but if you fail, remember, I told you so.")
- Global, all-encompassing accusations that use words such as *never*, *always*, *should*, and *ought*. ("You never listen"; "You always do this to me"; "You should be more considerate"; "You ought to know better.")
- An attempt to make your lover feel guilty. ("You know how much I count on you"; "This shows you don't really care"; "You're a fool; how could you?")
- An uncontrolled outburst of anger and yelling to intimidate your love partner. ("Look at what you've done now"; "This is the last straw"; "I hate you.")
- The use of old resentments as ammunition. ("This is just like the time you . . ."; "You're just like your mother"; "You've always been that way.")

EXERCISE

How do you contribute to a destructive argument? Which of the above "weapons" do you sometimes use? Be specific. What do you need to watch out for to avoid destructive arguing?

NEEDED: MUTUAL SUPPORT

He came home
after a bad day at the office
needing her support
a cup of hot tea
and reassurance
but he didn't tell her that

She also had a rough day
and needed to talk
a back rub
and some compassion
but she didn't say that

so instead
they had a fight

LOVE SECRET #14

THERE IS SUCH A THING AS A GOOD ARGUMENT

♦ If your intention is to communicate your hurt and desire for a specific change, an argument can be constructive. A good argument releases tension and facilitates an emotional breakthrough that can help your relationship evolve to a new level of understanding. An argument becomes constructive when you are committed to a positive outcome, and your anger is shaped by the following characteristics. It:

- Gets immediate attention through assertive but warm requests. ("We've got to talk now, I'm angry . . ."; "I'm upset and need to explain why . . ."; "I'm hurting, please give me your attention.")
- Communicates hurt using "I" statements. ("I feel let down, disappointed, hurt"; "I have trouble when you . . . I'd prefer if you would . . .")
- Communicates specific requests for change. ("I am hurt when you don't call me if you are going to be late; I am busy, too . . ."; "I am hurt when you ignore me at a party and I'd like to be introduced to your friends.")
- Leaves you open to your lover's feelings and point of view. ("I can see how you feel"; "I understand now my miscommunication.")
- Empowers both partners to change a destructive pattern through mutual cooperation. ("Since we both want . . . we'll need to watch out for . . ."; "I know you're trying and I appreciate it; what more can we do to solve this problem?")

EXERCISE

Give two specific examples of a good argument you had with your love partner and the benefits achieved. How did these confrontations help your relationship move to a new level of understanding? What did you do that helped make it a positive learning experience?

I DON'T LOVE HIM ANYMORE

I told myself,
I don't love him anymore
he hurt me
I hope he's hurting, too
I hope he suffers
terribly

And then I saw his face
drawn with exhaustion and pain
and felt worse
about his suffering
than about mine

Maybe I love him still?

WHEN YOU MAKE AN EMOTIONAL MISTAKE (EVERYBODY DOES), ACKNOWLEDGE IT AND APOLOGIZE

♦ Everybody and every love relationship "blows it" sometimes, despite the best intentions and wisdom in the world.

♦ Make sure your love is not some overidealized concept. Everybody makes "emotional mistakes." Acknowledge your errors as quickly as possible and find a way to reestablish heart-to-heart communication.

♦ Minor shortcomings or endearing weaknesses add humor to affection. Perfection is not necessary. Love allows room for disagreements, mistakes, and sadness. Love does mean learning to say, "I'm sorry."

♦ By virtue of being a human being, there will be times when you act irresponsible, stingy, incompetent, extravagant, a jerk, strange, hopeless, too aggressive, too sensitive, insensitive, impulsive, timid, rigid, manipulative, or controlling. Admit when you have been off the mark, petty, or out of control. Allow your partner to express his or her shock, anger, or disappointment, and then move on.

♦ The less harshly you judge yourself, the more accepting you become of others. The stronger and more secure your self-esteem becomes, the more willing you are to be yourself, and thereby encourage your loved ones to do the same.

EXERCISE

When you are hurt and vulnerable, how can your love partner help you to feel most accepted and understood? How can you best assist your love partner when he or she has blown it? How can he or she best assist you when you have blown it?

LIES!

I say to him
"Dear, all I want
is to stay home with you"
and I really mean it.

But when I'm called
to work here
or go there
or do this
or study that
I happily accept
to go wherever
and do whatever.

And I say to him
"I'm sorry, dear.
I wanted so much
to just stay home with you."
And I really mean it.

I do not know
which is the truth
What I say
or what I do?

FAVOR THE POSITIVE

◆ You can work wonders by overlooking negative remarks, while never failing to appreciate your love partner's good deeds. A smile or kind word is more potent than any threat, turmoil, or tantrum.

◆ Strive to be good-humored, considerate, optimistic, patient, and forgiving of your love partner's imperfections. What you place your attention on grows stronger. Favor the positive and it will grow.

◆ Most of us like not only to be loved, but also to be told that we are loved. Tell him tonight how much you hold him dear. Compliment her on a job well done or an outfit worn well. Share a heartfelt kiss.

◆ Mark Twain used to say that he could live for two months on a good compliment. He never did say whether it was one he received or one he gave. Kind words produce positive feelings not only in the recipient, but also in the sender. Learning to receive compliments graciously with a "thank you" allows both you and your partner to feel good.

◆ Talk happiness. No road is wholly rough; look for the places that are smooth and clear. Set aside a time and place to talk about your worries, fears, or problems. Deal with them at that time, as opposed to bringing up your negative emotions throughout the day.

EXERCISE

Especially for a couple that has fallen into bad habits, a good exercise is for each of you to list on a piece of paper ten specific things you like or appreciate about your love partner. Items must be positive and specific. For example, "I enjoyed our walk through the park last Sunday; our talk was very meaningful to me." Exchange papers and then briefly discuss each item. Keep to the positive.

PRIORITIES

We're working too hard
Accomplishing a lot but . . .
The time to play is passing us by.

We're in our separate worlds
Of creative concentration
It's wonderful but . . .
The time to live is passing us by.

We meet for meals
And speak of work
It's helpful but . . .
The time to know is passing us by.

We meet in bed
And go to sleep
It's restful but . . .
The time to love is passing us by.

GET UNSTUCK AND
LIGHTEN UP

♦ When we think of love, we usually think of passion and romance, rather than playfulness and laughter. Yet a shared joke, a knowing wink, and a sense of play adds much to love and intimacy.

♦ It is important to learn to laugh together; not at each other but with each other. We can giggle at our predictable behaviors, at our known foibles, at the wrong thing said to the wrong person at the wrong time. That laughter does not signal mocking or contempt, but understanding and love.

♦ Laughter is not only a great connector, it is also a great healer. You and your love partner can help each other step outside the melodrama. It doesn't take much to lighten up and change the energy.

♦ For instance, a loved one may come home after a rough day at work and take out his or her frustration by yelling at the kids or you. Instead of becoming angry and miserable, try to create some humor and fun. Imagine your grouchy partner as a warm and cuddly bear in need of a hug and love.

EXERCISE

If your partner were to be an item of food, what would he or she be? Why? Describe why you chose this particular food to represent your love partner. If your partner were to be an animal, what animal would he or she be? Again, describe why. Ask your love partner to make food and animal associations of you.

TOYS ARE US

Sometimes we are like
those little boxes
that fit so neatly
inside each other

Sometimes we are like
the colorful rings
that stack on a pole
on top of one another

Sometimes we are like
the little toy trains
that are coupled together
behind one another

Toys are us!

TAKE TIME FOR YOURSELF AND YOU'LL HAVE MORE LOVE TO GIVE YOUR PARTNER

♦ Is your internal motor running so fast that you are impatient with your love partner? Do you feel time pressure when you are trying to make love? If yes, you are suffering from stress, the most common dis-ease and dis-order of our time.

♦ Stress is a contagious dis-ease. One person staying calm can soothe another's hurt or angry heart. Hostility and emotional uptightness do not have to be met with resentment or irritation. It helps to be as compassionate as possible when your love partner is going through a high-stress period.

♦ Most people assume they can accomplish more in a given period than is actually possible. You and your love partner would be wise to allow extra time for things to go wrong or for new pressures to arise; they always do.

♦ Whenever possible, avoid making important decisions or taking action when you are emotionally upset. Your choices will be better if you wait until you are calm and centered.

♦ If you are stressed or running on empty your relationship will suffer. The more unfulfilled you feel, the more problems will arise. Take time to fill your cup; you'll have more to give to your love partner.

EXERCISE

If you find yourself irritable and angry when you and your lover are under stress, ask for a time-out. The purpose is not to avoid a necessary discussion but rather to take some time for each of you to relax and regain composure. You might say, "This argument is out of control. Let's take twenty minutes to cool down and unwind. Then we'll be calmer and more receptive to working it out." Or, "Thanks for your input. I'd like to give it careful thought during a twenty-minute time-out and talk about it later." This time-out can be used to go for a brisk walk or meditate and relax. A time-out is an opportunity to look at both sides of the issue, consider how you may have contributed to the problem, and develop creative solutions.

NO EXIT

If I don't have enough work
I get anxious
so I accept to do more
and then I have too much
and I get harried
and so I try to do less
but then I don't have enough
to keep me busy
so I get depressed
and I increase my work load
but then I can't manage it all
and I become frantic
so I decrease my responsibilities
and don't have enough work
so I get anxious . . .
Oh, shit!

YOU DESERVE APPRECIATION BUT SOMETIMES YOU MUST ASK FOR IT

♦ In a long-term relationship there is a tendency to give less acknowledgment to your lover's best qualities, such as generosity or the ability to compromise. Feeling taken for granted, couples often attack each other for becoming hard-hearted, selfish, and unfeeling. The best prescription for the hard-hearted is appreciation.

♦ Although it may seem uncomfortable at first, if you see your lover taking you for granted, it is your responsibility to request the love and appreciation you deserve. Don't just wait for an occasional compliment or drop hints about your needs. You deserve to be consistently and lovingly appreciated, but sometimes you must ask for it.

♦ It is a good habit for lovers to find a regular time—over a cup of coffee, at day's end, or else when going out for dinner—to acknowledge each other. You might take turns using phrases like, "The best thing about our love relationship is . . ."; "The things I love most about you are . . ." No one ever tires of hearing how much they are loved.

♦ Each of us thrives on different kinds of appreciation. A beautiful woman may receive frequent attention for her physical attributes, but what she may really need is acknowledgment for being competent, intelligent, and effective. A person who is highly successful may get enough acknowledgment for his or her career performance, but what he or she really needs to hear is that the love will be there whether he or she succeeds or fails.

EXERCISE

Starting right now and for the next week, share five appreciations a day. For example: "That was an excellent dinner you made"; "You are so much fun to be with"; "I really enjoy it when you sing and play the piano for me"; "Our love means a great deal to me"; "Having you by my side gives me strength"; "I admire how honest and straightforward you are in business"; "You have an excellent memory"; "Your enthusiasm is contagious"; "Thank you for being available to listen."

THE WHOLE IS MORE THAN THE SUM OF ITS PARTS

Of course I love you
and I love me, too
but most of all
I love "us"

I love the "we," the you *and* me,
the relationship,
the way each one
is enriched by the other

I am smarter
when you're around
you are braver
when I am there
We find each other
beautiful, brilliant
and great fun

We are each the other's parent
each the other's child
each the other's partner, colleague
friend, consultant, lover,
and accomplice

You tend to be serious
I'm rather spontaneous
you make me think more
I make you laugh more

Of course I love you
and I love me, too
but most of all I love "us"

A LOVE RELATIONSHIP BUILT ON EXCITEMENT ALONE IS DOOMED TO FAILURE

◆ When you become romantically involved, you are on an intense adrenaline and endorphin high. Romantic love can be very exciting; sex ups the ante even more. However, the body can keep the flow of adrenaline and endorphins going for just so long. Soon you become exhausted, depressed, or bored.

◆ Almost everyone has experienced the physical sensations of romance:

- a pounding of the heart
- rapid, shallow breathing
- butterflies in the stomach
- goose bumps, chills
- tingling, trembling
- sexual excitement

◆ What most of us call love is the intense exhilaration of falling in love. But then, as the romantic high becomes less intense, you grow disappointed. You may become disillusioned and yearn for a new Mr. or Ms. Magic to come along.

◆ Many people are addicted to romance. No wonder there is so much disappointment in love; no wonder so many marriages fail. Relationships built on excitement alone are doomed to failure.

◆ Romantic love is not "bad"; indeed, it is a beautiful experience. But stars and rockets do not a lifetime make. The rush and elation of romantic love must give rise to a wise and mature loving. A balance of excitement and quiet pleasures allows a relationship to grow.

EXERCISE

Have you ever been addicted to the excitement and rush of romance? What were the consequences?

DISAPPOINTMENT

I like it when you're flirting
but not with my friends
I like your silences
but not at dinner parties
I like it when you're neat
but not when you're compulsive
I like it when you're casual
but not disorganized
I like you to be outgoing
but not a social butterfly
I like you to be quiet
but not withdrawn
I like you to be athletic
but not a body builder

I like you to be perfect
according to my stereotypes
And fit exactly
my image of a perfect mate

JEALOUSY IS SOMETIMES THE SUREST WAY TO GET RID OF THE VERY PERSON YOU ARE AFRAID OF LOSING

◆ Jealousy is sometimes the surest way to get rid of the very person you are afraid of losing. Conversation turns into an inquisition: "Where were you?"; "What did he (she) look like?"; "How do I know you're not lying?" Excess jealousy can destroy the very love it seeks to protect.

◆ When two people in a love relationship are complete within themselves they do not experience the love they have for others as diminishing, detracting, or threatening to the love they share. They are free of the fear and insecurity that can give rise to destructive jealousy.

◆ If your partner is having an interesting conversation with a member of the opposite sex at a party, that is no reason for jealousy. However, if he or she is flirting, that is another matter. Your hurt feelings need to be addressed, not in the heat of the moment but when both of you can discuss the impact of the behavior on the other partner.

◆ It is an irony that the more possessive you are, the more love you demand, the less you receive, while the more freedom you give, the less you demand, the more love you will receive. A true love relationship can never be held together by demanding "shoulds" and "should nots." Heavy demands are a self-fulfilling prophecy that eventually make the other person go away.

EXERCISE

Describe the specific times when you felt: (1) most jealous, (2) most emotionally suffocated, and (3) most free.

EXTRAMARITAL AFFAIR

Having an extramarital affair
is like eating dessert
when you're on a diet:
the pleasure is short
the guilt is long
and the habit can
ruin your life

FORGIVE YOURSELF FOR NOT BEING PERFECT

♦ Too many people still believe that they are innately sinful or evil; that the nature of life is to suffer. Unnecessary guilt may be the result of inappropriate parental anger or frequently being told you are "bad." As a result of internalizing a harsh inner critic, people wind up treating themselves worse than their parents ever did.

♦ Innocent until proven guilty is a fundamental principle. But you would never know it by looking at how some people treat themselves and their loved ones. Whenever they have an occasion for personal gratification or relaxed fun, they cut their joy short. They treat themselves like prisoners who steal pleasure to which they have no right.

♦ More commonly, people suffer from an endless array of mini-guilts, punishing themselves with self-inflicted "buzzes" of anxiety. Mini-guilts are often the result of internalized "shoulds." Learn to substitute a softer, lighter, "It would be nice if . . ." for your harsh, demanding "shoulds." Enthusiasm, enjoyment, and fun are every bit as important to living and loving as care and responsibility.

♦ To overcome unnecessary guilt, you may have to give up feeling sorry for yourself, straining to be someone you are not, hiding the parts of yourself you fear are unacceptable, and worrying about what others think. You may have to forgive yourself for not being perfect, and stop expecting superhuman feats from yourself. Indeed, you may have to accept yourself as you are instead of what you think you should be.

EXERCISE

The next time you engage in self-putdowns for not living up to some unrealistic standard, ask yourself, "Who am I trying to please? Whose approval am I desperately seeking?" It's time to set these punishing expectations aside and make your own rules and standards.

REMORSE AND REGRET

Is it better to have
remorse than regret?
Remorse is for what you did
and wish you hadn't
Regret is for what you did not do
and wish you had.

I have always preferred
sins of commission
over those of omission,
I would rather act and risk
than not act and wish I had

NO PAIN, NO GAIN

♦ Whenever you take a new step and venture into unknown emotional territory, you are bound to experience some anxiety. Some fear is natural when you commit to a new relationship, or confront a problem in your marriage.

♦ By remaining stuck you can try avoiding reality. By refusing to work on a difficulty in your relationship, you can convince yourself that the relationship is basically sound and will last. Sooner or later this bubble of self-delusion will burst.

♦ Too often the words "wish," "hope," and "maybe" are sedatives you administer to yourself to numb your sensitivity to your emotional realities. Substitute "I will make my marriage work" for "maybe my marriage will work out."

♦ Stop thinking of yourself as fragile. You won't realize how strong you are until you stop putting up with problems in your love relationship and take some steps toward change.

♦ Developing psychological strengths is just like developing a musical or athletic ability. The more you exercise, the stronger you become.

E XERCISE

What were the three most painful events in your life? What did you learn from those difficult times that caused you to be the person you are today?

LOSE/WIN

I have known the path of
failure
frustration
disappointment
defeat

Because I have taken a chance on
winning
succeeding
achieving

It takes a lot of the first
to get some of the second

A BROKEN HEART REQUIRES AS MUCH CARE AS A BROKEN LEG

◆ A broken heart requires at least as much care as a broken bone. With proper care you can be confident that you will heal. The same powerful forces that mend a broken bone will heal your emotional pain, but a wounded heart needs time and proper care to heal.

◆ Be with the pain. Admit you're hurting. The greater the loss the more time you will take to heal. Don't worry about having ups and downs; these are a sign that you're healing.

◆ You are more fragile now, there is no shame in that, so take it easy. Crying is a natural release. Remember you are not alone. You can't be a human being without suffering loss.*

EXERCISE

Here is some emotional first aid for a broken heart:

DOS	DON'TS
• Stay calm; treat yourself gently.	• Don't panic.
• Recognize your injury.	• Don't deny the hurt.
• Be with the pain.	• Don't blame yourself.
• Take time to heal.	• Don't dwell on the negative.
• Rest, nurture yourself.	• Don't abuse alcohol or drugs.
• Accept comfort from friends and family.	• Don't stay isolated.
• Stick to a routine.	• Don't create more chaos.
• Take care in making important decisions.	• Don't make impulsive judgments; be wary of love on the rebound.
• Accept understanding and support.	• Don't be afraid to ask for help.
• Anticipate a positive outcome.	• Don't lose faith.

*For more assistance please read *How to Survive the Loss of a Love* by Melba Colgrove, Ph.D., Harold H. Bloomfield, M.D., and Peter McWilliams, Prelude Press, Los Angeles, 1991.

LOST AND FOUND

Losing someone
is not only
losing a loved one
it is losing
a friend
a colleague
a mentor
a parent
a child
it is losing
a way of life

it is hard to believe
at that moment
that a new way of life
is waiting
to be found

LOVE'S GREAT DAMPENER IS CHRONIC FATIGUE

◆ Most of us take on more than it is humanly possible to accomplish in any given day. Sooner or later, as we try to cram more and more into less and less time the result is chronic fatigue, the complaint heard most in doctors' offices.

◆ The signs and symptoms of chronic fatigue are as follows:

- dullness
- pouches under the eyes
- poor muscle tone
- pasty, pale complexion
- lack of spontaneity
- tendency to be bored or depressed
- fear, tension, and anxiety
- decreased cooperativeness
- less acceptance of constructive criticism
- irritability, temper outbursts
- lowered attention span
- impaired recent memory
- decreased libido (sex drive)
- insomnia, waking up tired
- physical complaints, such as headache or back pain
- decreased interest in personal care
- drug and alcohol abuse
- decreased general health and satisfaction

◆ Is it any wonder that chronic fatigue is such an inhibitor of love and well-being? All growth is based on optimum cycles of rest and activity. The biggest hazard to satisfaction and love is to become burned out.

EXERCISE

What symptoms of chronic fatigue do you suffer from? What do you need to do about it? Review your life-style and personal habits.

I'M ALWAYS TIRED

Household chores
are never done
there is always
one more thing
that needs to be cleaned,
cooked, mended
or put away.

Work is also never done
there is always
one more item
that needs to be studied,
written, calculated
or filed away.

I'm always catching up
but I'm never "caught up"
when I think I have finished,
terminated, accomplished, resolved
love starts to feel like
one more thing
that needs to get done.

DEPRESSION IMPAIRS THE ABILITY TO LOVE AND BE LOVED AND IS TOO OFTEN OVERLOOKED

◆ Most people are unaware that an inability to love and be loved, a lack of sexual passion, or chronic irritability may be the biological result of depressive illness. All too often depression is misdiagnosed or overlooked.

◆ Almost as painful as being depressed is being the love partner of someone suffering from this disorder. No matter how hard you try to be intimate and stimulate passion, nothing seems to work.

◆ It is sometimes hard to recognize when you or someone close to you is depressed. All depressions are not the same; they vary considerably in duration and degree. While its symptoms may vary, depression always impairs the ability to love.

◆ The primary symptoms of depression are a pessimistic or critical attitude, a diminished capacity for love and affection, boredom, loss of concentration, difficulty in decision making, neglect of personal appearance, low self-esteem, outbursts of rage, insomnia, and excess guilt.

◆ Depression can contribute to compulsive gambling, eating disorders, alcohol and drug abuse, and a wide array of physical complaints.

◆ Biological depression results from a biochemical imbalance in the brain. Antidepressants, taken as prescribed by a psychiatrist, are nonaddictive and often effective. Psychotherapy may also be important. See your doctor for a thorough evaluation.

EXERCISE

Have you or your love partner ever been seriously depressed? What were the circumstances and symptoms? How did depression inhibit the ability to love or be loved?

THE BLUES

Sometimes I'm angry and upset
and I don't know why
I just have this short fuse
I blow up for nothing
become nasty, impatient
and give the nicest people
a hard time

I hate myself that way
but the strong feelings are there
just under the surface
ready to come out
and hit the next person
I see

Then I feel terrible
feel guilty, I apologize
and can't understand
what's gotten into me

YOUR UNFINISHED BUSINESS WITH PARENTS AFFECTS YOUR ADULT LOVE LIFE

◆ Was your parents' marriage an ideal model of what you want in a love relationship? Most people answer no; they desire much more. The fact is, however, the state of your parents' marriage can exert a major unseen influence on the quality of your own love relationship.

◆ Below are some warning signs of unfinished business with your parents.* Do any of the following apply to you?

- You explode in anger over small matters and later regret what you said.
- You feel left out, unappreciated, or taken for granted.
- You poke fun at or make spiteful comments to those you love.
- You abuse alcohol, drugs, or food.
- You suffer from fears of rejection, disapproval, or abandonment.
- You create "arm's-length" intimacy.
- You harbor regrets or resentments from childhood.

EXERCISE

To discover the unseen influences of your upbringing on your adult love life, explore the following: Would you like to have a marriage just like your parents had? In what ways are you like your mother or father? In what ways are you different from them? How have childhood arguments and power struggles affected your adult love life? How do you act out these old patterns and power struggles? Give specific examples.

*For more assistance please read *Making Peace With Your Parents* by Harold H. Bloomfield, M.D., with Leonard Felder, Ph.D., Ballantine, New York, 1985.

I SOUND JUST LIKE MY MOTHER

Sometimes I sound just like my mother,
and I'm shocked
at what crosses my lips.
I used to think,
I'll never say things like that,
but now and then I do.

Sometimes I catch
a glimpse of myself in the mirror,
and I'm shocked.
I look just like my mother.

Is this her immortality
that continues to live through me?

YOU MAY EXPERIENCE WITH YOUR LOVE PARTNER THE HURT, FEAR, AND ANGER YOU FELT AS A CHILD

♦ The psychological importance of working through painful resentments cannot be underestimated. Not to release and rise above suppressed feelings of hurt and anger is to remain imprisoned by them.

♦ No matter how we try to justify our resentments or believe we have the past "handled," we suffer emotional wounds and even ill health from any unfinished business of the heart.

♦ When you have unfinished business with a parent, you may at times experience with your love partner the same feelings of guilt, hurt, anger, rage, or entrapment you felt as a child.

♦ Fulfillment in your current love relationship depends on successfully healing and learning from past hurts. Unless you are willing to do so, similar conflicts may appear in the future.

♦ You don't need to leave a good relationship simply because your partner has restimulated painful memories or your old emotional tapes. To the contrary, you can heal your unresolved hurts and have an adult love relationship that becomes a corrective emotional experience.

EXERCISE

Here is a simple but powerful tool. Whenever you get furious, resentful, or emotionally withdrawn from a loved one, with very little or no provocation, ask yourself what the person may be doing that reminds you of your mother, father, or an ex-lover. Then take a few deep breaths and remind yourself over and over that this person is your love partner and not some person from your past. You can throw off your past negative emotional conditioning and then choose a healthier, more loving response.

NEEDED: BODY PARTS

A brain to pick
A shoulder to cry on
A kick in the pants

A hand to hold
An arm to lean on
A step to follow

WHAT YOU BELIEVE TO BE SO, BECOMES SO; YOU GET THE LOVE RELATIONSHIP YOU THINK YOU DESERVE

♦ Sigmund Freud described the "repetition compulsion": Whatever was experienced as traumatic, deficient, or incomplete in your childhood, there is a tendency to re-create. When a child feels deeply hurt, rejected, and ignored, this may begin an inferiority complex or self-hate.

♦ The search for power, prestige, and admiration may be a means of seeking a parent's—the world's—approval. Perfectionism, compulsive overachievement, may be an unconscious means of seeking the attention missing in childhood. No matter what you do, it is never enough.

♦ Although there may be an innate tendency to repeat your childhood dramas you can also work through them. What you need is an understanding of how your upbringing affected you, what negative attitudes you may have internalized, and how to change these outdated emotional habits.

EXERCISE

These questions can help you to recognize and rise above old childhood conflicts:

How did your mother and father treat you? Did either make degrading comments that left you feeling inferior? What specific statements did they make that you've never forgiven them for? Did you feel humiliated, controlled, or withdrawn? Did you try even harder to be "good" or become rebellious? What negative beliefs and poor images about yourself did you internalize that show up in your adult love life?

MOVING BEYOND

I have been hurt
many times in my life
I have been treated unfairly
I have been ignored,
discounted, demeaned
and I have often lost
my self-confidence
I have doubted
others' intentions
I have learned to mistrust,
to be cynical

But none of this
should apply to you
nor even to me anymore
none of it should spoil
our relationship
I need to trust you
and be loving
in spite of the past
I need to trust you
and love you
because of the past

FORGIVING YOUR LOVE PARTNER PRIMARILY BENEFITS YOU

♦ Forgiveness doesn't mean forgetting, whitewashing the wrong, or being a martyr. Forgiveness means choosing to let go, move on, and favor the positive.

♦ The first step is to release your hurt and anger safely and constructively, without dumping on your partner. Rather than piling accusations on your partner, express your pain in a way that can be most appreciated: "I felt hurt when . . ." or "I feel insecure about . . ." are better than accusatory "you did" or "you bastard" statements.

♦ The second step is the acknowledgment that both of you can grow from the incident. Don't be afraid to admit how you might have contributed to the miscommunication and upset. The issue is not to blame or find fault, but to learn and grow.

♦ Last, forgiveness must include the expression of love, trust, and intimacy. The more you can express your feelings of tenderness and commitment, the more easily your partner can acknowledge your pain.

♦ Forgive not just for your love partner but for you—your peace of mind, your health, and the quality of your love relationship.*

EXERCISE

What incidents from your adult life do you still need to make peace with? What resentments in your love relationship have you been holding on to that it is now time to forgive?

*For more assistance please read *Lifemates* by Harold H. Bloomfield, M.D., and Sirah Vettese, Ph.D., with Robert B. Kory, Signet, New York, 1992.

You Hurt Me

You hurt me!
If you did not mean to
then I must wonder
what is in me
that responds with pain

You hurt me!
And if you meant to
then I will wonder
what is in you
that makes you want to hurt me

WATER YOUR FAMILY ROOTS TO ENJOY LOVE'S FRUITS

♦ Remember your parents saying, "You'll never understand what it's like to be a parent until you are one yourself"? Everything comes full circle. Only when you first become a parent can you fully appreciate the major responsibility—and privilege—of raising a child.

♦ Adolescent turmoil and rebellion sometimes lead to a disruption, or even cutting off, of parental ties. As the noise settles down, rekindle the relationship. Now that you are an adult, it is time to make peace with your parents.

♦ Speak at length with your family elders. Have them tell you of their parents, childhood, customs, and times. You'll gain a deeper appreciation of your history, traditions, and roots. You will also gain a richer understanding of yourself.

♦ Hold a family reunion, even if your aunt Agnes is a little flaky and you can't stand your cousin Morris. In this age of families being spread all over the world, there is great power and love in a gathering of the clan.

♦ Get together with your childhood friends. Your "blood relatives" don't just end with your second cousins; we are all blood relatives in the human family.

EXERCISE

In what ways have you broken away from your roots? In what ways have you taken on the best values of your family and cultural roots? What patterns, issues, and struggles from your family of origin continue to affect your adult life and love relationships? Visit your family this year; consider interviewing your parents and other elders on audio- or videotape. What will be your family legacy?

FAMILIES

Families may be those
who have borne you
and families may be those
who have grown you
and families may be those
who have known you
but no matter what you do
real families
will never disown you

KNOW WHEN TO GET HELP

♦ You or your love partner should consider psychotherapy if:

- Your love relationship is repeatedly frustrating.
- You're not feeling good about yourself most of the time.
- You're seeking solace in a liquor bottle, drugs, or a make-believe world.
- There is no joy in your life or there is persistent emotional pain.
- You and your love partner regularly get stuck in bitter, hostile conflicts.
- You feel blocked off from your feelings or feel under perpetual strain.
- You're in a severe emotional crisis, and wise friends and family support won't do.
- You are shut down sexually or feel chronically turned off by your love partner.
- You're not living up to your potential and want more out of life.
- You are afraid that you may act on suicidal thoughts or rage.
- You may be suffering from a psychiatric disorder.

EXERCISE

Whom would you call in an emotional crisis? Who among your family and friends is the most helpful person to talk to?

THE KEY TO HAPPINESS?

If rich and thin
were the keys to happiness
there would not be
so many thin rich people
in psychiatrists' offices

A LOVING ATTITUDE
IS CONTAGIOUS

♦ How do you feel about yourself? There's a big difference between just feeling pretty good about yourself and the unrestricted appetite for living that comes from loving yourself fully.

♦ Most of us have been taught that we have to strain to become more loving, try harder to deserve more love. Don't push, complain, or denounce yourself. You're good enough to love just the way you are.

♦ Love of self is the opposite of selfishness. The selfish person lacks self-love and so stays chronically needy. This endless "shopping list" of needs, demands, and expectations fails to bring him or her lasting satisfaction. The cure for selfishness is more love, especially from within.

♦ When you can accept and love yourself, you can be yourself without pretense. That gives others the freedom to be themselves. If you can be open, honest, and loving, others will respond in kind.

♦ Loving yourself fully is a key to taking advantage of all your possibilities. It is indispensable to your own dynamism and creativity. It is basic to your enthusiasm for life.

EXERCISE

Make a list of ten qualities you love most in yourself. Give specific examples. What are your greatest gifts?

I Think You're Wonderful

You are intelligent and loving
fun to be with
and always there

You're understanding
and sympathetic
always giving me good advice

You are sensitive
and very honest
and always know the way I feel

You are aware
of today's issues
and always trying to be fair

You're wise and kind
you're wonderful
yet what I like best about you
is that you think
I'm wonderful, too.

NO ONE CAN MAKE YOU FEEL INFERIOR WITHOUT YOUR CONSENT

♦ You may say that you feel good about yourself, but your behavior may speak otherwise. Which of these forms of low self-worth apply to you?

- Feeling embarrassed about your abilities. ("It wasn't skill, just luck." "Today was just a good day.")
- Giving credit to others when you really deserve it. ("Martha did all the work, I just drew a plan." You write a report and let your superior put his or her name on it.)
- Failing to stand up for what you believe. (You criticize the President's policy; someone counters with a barrage of statistics; you back down.)
- Passing up an opportunity for fun because you feel you don't deserve it. (Friends invite you to the beach/movies/park but you stay home and work, even though you need a few hours of relaxation.)
- Saying yes when you want to say no in order to be a "good guy/gal." (A friend asks you to do an errand and you agree, even though it's really not convenient and you feel angry about it.)

♦ Do you indulge in any of these self-negating acts? If you do, you have a clue to your inner deforming mirrors and how you are inadvertently training others to see and treat you. As Eleanor Roosevelt recognized "no one can make you feel inferior without your consent."

EXERCISE

In what ways are you your own worst critic? What specific thoughts and behaviors reveal hidden feelings of inadequacy? How do you put yourself down or fail to take the credit you deserve?

UNAFRAID

If I am small and weak,
then I act big and strong
lest I be found out
and not be loved.

When I am big and strong,
then I can ask for help—
unafraid of what they will think,
unafraid to seem weak,
Unafraid.

TRUST YOUR INNER VOICE

♦ Most of us tie up enormous energy suppressing our feelings and trying to be someone we're not. There is a gulf between the mask we show the world and the self we keep hidden within.

♦ To the extent that we have stress, guilt, and shame in our mental storehouse, we tend to hide behind our social roles and masks. The true self is felt to be weak, ugly, or afraid, and so a wall of "defense mechanisms" is constructed. Such a psychic life may be safe, but it is also lonely; love is locked out.

♦ Make a habit of periodically "checking in" with your inner voice to see if you are putting on a mask or hiding something important. You may be masking your real emotions and need to check in when you feel shut down, inhibited, or off the mark.

♦ Everyone has an inner voice, but most of us are only dimly aware of it. The inner voice is the innermost dimension of the self. It communicates in the subtle, intuitive language of the heart.

EXERCISE

Take some quiet time daily to become more familiar with your inner voice. Although your inner voice is natural, you must cultivate your ability to hear it. The inner voice is sometimes able to know what you can't rationally explain. As you get better at tuning into and trusting your inner voice, you will experience more joy, creativity, and love.

Not Halloween

We all wear masks
and sit inside a shell
to keep our nerve endings protected
our hopes, fears, and hang-ups, hidden
our prides and prejudices,
irrationalities and cry buttons,
from hanging out
for everyone to stare at or step upon.

We wear the masks
and sit in our shells
at work, at church,
at home, at parties.
The masks change
depending on the people we meet
some masks are made of cardboard—
impenetrable;
others of gauze—
waiting to be seen through.
And under all the masks
and inside all the shells
live people who are worried
about health, looks, money,
family, and happiness
anxious whether
others will like them or hate them,
or worse, simply ignore them.

So I will take off my mask
if you come out of your shell.
The question is
Who goes first?

NO MATTER HOW GOOD OR COMMITTED YOUR LOVE RELATIONSHIP, YOU WILL ALWAYS BE "SINGLE"

♦ No matter how committed your love relationship or marriage, you'll always be "single," as well as part of a couple. Love is a special, intense connection, but it is not an answer to all or even most individual problems.

♦ The unspoken contract for many love relationships and marriages is, "I'll be responsible for your happiness, and you be responsible for mine." While this may sound loving, no one can make you happy except you.

♦ Wishing for your partner to make you happy is doubly frustrating. Not only do you fail to take responsibility for your own happiness, but trying to change your partner is futile. The more you try to change your love partner, the more likely he or she is to feel rejected and unloved, and therefore, resistant to change.

♦ A quality relationship is not made up of partners who try to rescue each other or become emotionally entangled in codependency. Only when both partners are striving to be full and complete within themselves can love and happiness blossom.

♦ You can make requests, be candid, and give feedback, but manipulation of your lover to meet your needs is a prescription for disaster. Change only comes about because your love partner wants it.

EXERCISE

How have you been trying to get your love partner to provide you with a feeling or experience you must ultimately provide yourself? Do you ever try to make your love partner feel guilty or responsible if you are not getting what you want?

ARE YOU MORE IF I'M LESS?

Are you more if I'm less?
Do I breathe your air
or fly in your space?
When I take up more room,
do you become constrained?
Do you value me more
when I'm beholden to you?
Do you value me less
when I'm free and I soar?
Are you less if I'm more?

YOUR HAPPINESS IS PRIMARILY UP TO YOU, NOT YOUR LOVE PARTNER

♦ You have been given responsibility for caring, nurturing, and raising at least one person, and that is you. The better you take care of yourself, the more you will have to give to others.

♦ Below is a list of specific ways to keep the child in you alive and playing:

- Talk to yourself gently, with affection.
- Trust your inner voice and intuition.
- Develop your potential and creativity.
- Give yourself the benefit of the doubt.
- Forgive yourself for your faults; get over that guilty feeling.
- Play and have fun—lots of it.
- Develop and live by your own code of ethics.
- Know when to say *yes*, and when to say *no*.
- Take responsible risks for your own advancement.
- Enjoy winning, but don't despair at losing.
- Affirm yourself; let yourself succeed.
- Feel pleasure fully; know you deserve it.
- Love your body and your sexuality.
- "Yes," give yourself permission.
- Surround yourself with life-supporting people and ideas.
- Surround yourself with beauty, especially the natural.
- Take in the love, affection, and compliments of others.
- Stay physically fit.

EXERCISE

From the above list, what are five specific ways you could love and take care of yourself better? What would be a specific change or program by which you might start doing that?

TOMORROW I WILL CHANGE

Tomorrow I will change
turn a new leaf
become this new person

I will exercise before breakfast
not eat cookies between meals
not fret over trivialities
not run about
getting upset
that I'm not getting
everything done

Tomorrow I will change.

I say this every day.

THERE IS NO BARRIER TO FEELING ATTRACTIVE, ONLY YOUR BELIEF

♦ If you judge your body and appearance harshly, you send out messages that say, "Don't notice me," or "Without makeup I'm a mess." Such self-criticism spurs others to see you as unattractive; your self-criticism becomes in essence a self-fulfilling prophecy.

♦ You don't have to be young, gorgeous, or pencil-slim to radiate sex appeal. When your posture, eye contact, facial expressions, clothing, and attitude reflect self-confidence, a lover will also feel good about your appearance. There is no barrier other than your belief to feeling sexy and attractive.

♦ Learning fully to accept and appreciate the way you look isn't easy. Everyone seems to have something to change. What is your complaint? Is it your hips, belly, butt, thighs, nose, complexion, teeth, hairline, or posture? Most of us deprecate ourselves for one or more physical characteristics, attempting to look like some media image.

♦ Anxiety about keeping a youthful appearance has become epidemic. Why can't we look at the physical signs of aging with as much pride as we have for memorabilia, scrapbooks, and treasures?*

EXERCISE

To feel more attractive, work on turning your "what ifs" into "so what ifs." For example:

What if I have wrinkles?
So what if I have wrinkles? It's a souvenir of my wisdom.

What if someone thinks I'm too old?
So what if someone thinks I'm too old? It's their loss.

---

*For more assistance please read *Making Peace With Yourself* by Harold H. Bloomfield, M.D., with Leonard Felder, Ph.D., Ballantine, New York, 1986.

WRONG CENTURY

If I lived in the time of
Rembrandt or Rubens or Renoir
When women had full breasts,
large buttocks, and big thighs
where dimples and folds
were considered beautiful
If I were living then
I would be much too thin

But I live in the time of
Vogue and *Cosmopolitan*
and so I'm too fat!

JUST AS DISSATISFACTION WITH YOURSELF IS CONTAGIOUS, SO IS ENTHUSIASM

♦ How do you feel about your body? You might say you aren't overly concerned with your looks, yet what happens when your love partner stares at someone who is especially attractive? How do you feel when you notice signs you are putting on weight or getting older? How confident are you about being seen in your bathing suit or undressing in front of your love partner?

♦ When you look at photographs of yourself, do you criticize your appearance mercilessly, or do you sometimes avoid having a love partner take your picture in the first place? How much time and money do you spend trying to make yourself look more youthful, slim, and attractive? Do you ever truly reach the point of being satisfied?

♦ Body image is important to loving yourself fully. Everybody seems to have something they would like to change but can't. Learning to accept and appreciate every part of your body—warts, wrinkles, and all—is a tremendously liberating experience. Find things about your body that you like; never mind the flaws.

♦ Posture is important; learn to stand straight. Overcoming your "slump" will require thought and practice. Walking around tall and erect—back straight, chin up, shoulders back, pelvis tucked under—will improve your self-esteem.

EXERCISE

Stand nude in front of a full-length mirror. What parts of your body do you like best? Which arouse a sense of shame or weakness? Now look into the mirror and say, "I love you." Say it several times, out loud. At first you may feel strange, embarrassed, or foolish—but do it. Say again, "I love you," and your name. Resistances will come up; don't turn your head away in shame. Love away any felt weakness or "flaw" in each part of your body. Keep loving yourself out loud until you see yourself with a relaxed, happy expression. Bravo!

BODIES

Some bodies are made
for bathing suits
**others look best
in formals**

Some bodies are made
for very tight pants
**others must wear
skirts**

Some bodies are made
for mannish suits
**others for
frilly blouses**

Some bodies are made
for hats and gloves
**others live in
jeans**

Some bodies are made
for fashion
**mine is made
for love**

FITNESS GIVES YOU ENERGY FOR LOVING FULLY

♦ Radiant health is a fundamental source of joy and love. Dullness and inertia of the body inhibit free emotional flow, lovemaking, and overall mental functioning. Physical fitness allows for the full pleasure of being alive and loving others.

♦ You are constricting your capacity for love and joy if you lack energy and vitality. Getting fit will not only help you to avoid illness and premature aging, but more important, to feel optimally alive.

♦ The most recent scientific evidence suggests strongly that health today is largely a matter of choice. You decide whether you are going to be fit. You determine whether your diet includes wholesome foods low in fat, sugar, salt, caffeine, and alcohol, or whether you eat without restraint. You decide whether to smoke or not, or to exercise.

♦ Your doctor can help you design a program to lose weight, stop smoking, decrease your alcohol intake, or get into shape, but your active participation is the vital ingredient. Change will come slowly, and your enthusiasm may at times plateau, but stick to a systematic health program and benefits will accrue.

♦ Mind and body are not separate. Emotional tension shows up in changes of bodily functioning, such as muscular rigidity and lower energy. A healthy body provides you with greater vitality.

EXERCISE

What do you need to do to become more fit?

FOOD

I have willpower
for everything
except for what's fattening.
Comes food
and I can't resist.
I will wait five minutes
talking to myself
then eat it anyway—
and even take second helpings
kicking myself all along
for having no willpower.
Help!

EXERCISE

Any excuse not to do it . . .
A slight morning backache
is a welcome impediment
The usual one is
"No time now, I'm late already"
Although I feel better all day
if I exercise in the morning
I manage not to
and luxuriate in bed
feeling deliciously guilty
Another fifteen minutes
Really believing that
"I'll start tomorrow for sure."

APPRECIATE YOURSELF
AS YOU ARE AS A BASIS
FOR CHANGE

♦ There is no one here but just us folks. We are all equal. The yardsticks by which we measure and compare ourselves are always too narrow to account for all the differences that make each one of us unique.

♦ Feeling good about yourself does not lead to self-preoccupation. It is the lack of good feelings about yourself that leads to self-absorption. You have to appreciate yourself exactly as you are, including your weak spots and vulnerabilities, as a basis for lasting change.

♦ If you resist and hate parts of yourself, negative habits are more likely to persist. That doesn't mean you can't actively and vigorously improve yourself, but it is best done, and the results will be most enduring, when it is done with a modicum of self-love. What you resist, persists; what you accept, lightens.

♦ The less harshly you judge yourself, the more accepting you become of others. We often criticize in others things we can't stand in ourselves.

EXERCISE

You can increase your self-esteem with affirmations. Affirmations are positive thoughts that you consciously choose to implant within your consciousness to produce a desirable result. For example, repeat to yourself out loud the affirmation, "I like myself; I approve of myself; I am a lovable person." Write down this affirmation for the next week before sleep, on awakening, and whenever you feel down. Just as you can weight lift to build up the muscles in your body, you can use these affirmations to build up a weakened self-esteem. It is essential to practice regularly until your self-talk becomes more spontaneously less critical and more supportive.

THE OK PERSON SEAL OF APPROVAL

I am always working on
my "OK Person Seal of Approval"
which must be earned
on a continuous basis
the criteria being:

a spotless home
with gourmet meals
fashionable clothes
a devoted husband
well-behaved children
flowers in the house
time for friends
knowledgeable about
politics and art
and the latest brain research

Will I ever earn
that "OK Person Seal of Approval"?

Even my mother says
I'm improving
I call her every day
I pay my bills on time
save for a rainy day
take my vitamins
stay on a diet
exercise every day
raise money for
the most worthwhile causes
Trying to be OK enough to earn
my "OK PERSON SEAL OF APPROVAL"

ALL GROWTH IS THE INTEGRATION OF SEEMINGLY OPPOSITE VALUES

♦ Develop and assert your personal power; take full responsibility for your happiness and well-being. Power doesn't mean being hostile, aggressive, or coercive; it means being confident, self-actualizing, and free.

♦ Women especially need to feel more comfortable with self-determination. Personal power does not require straining to be a superman or superwoman; it is a natural result of total personality development. Get into a self-improvement habit: body, intellect, emotional skills, relationships, and spirit.

♦ Balance is important. Psychological growth is the integration of seemingly opposite values. Don't develop one area of your personality at the cost of another. The concert pianist needs to engage in sports; the athlete needs to go to a concert.

♦ Your creativity and personal power, not just hard work, are the sources of great success. The most valuable work you do may be done in as little as five minutes—a brilliant idea, a pivotal decision, a simple solution, a telephone call. In those five minutes you can accomplish more than you can shuffling papers for twenty-four hours. When you relax and have fun, it gives you time to become inspired.

EXERCISE

What steps must you take to unfold your creative power and achieve greater balance in your life? Be specific.

EMPOWERMENT

First:
there must be power
which we feel

Next:
there must be power
which we wield

Then:
there can be power
which we share

WHAT YOU PLACE ATTENTION ON GROWS STRONGER

♦ Whatever you put your attention upon consistently will inevitably gain a stronger influence in your life. You are the creator of your experience. You are responsible for your life and choices—not your love partner, not your parents, not society.

♦ This is not to suggest that you should force yourself to have only positive thoughts. Life is not just meant to be a continuous experience of love and joy. Negative thoughts play a role; they reveal problems and issues that need attention.

♦ The point is to be in charge of your thoughts and feelings; to exercise choice. Do your thoughts and feelings serve you well? Do they work for or against you? Or have they become "psycho-sclerotic"—rigid, automatic, and mechanical?

♦ If all you pay attention to is warts and wrinkles, pretty soon that's what you see. If you focus excessively on what's "missing" in your relationship, you will remain dissatisfied. You can choose to be satisfied in your life and love relationships most of the time, as a result of your own enthusiasm, passion, and humor.

♦ Problems can be seen as opportunities to tap into your stamina, creativity, and courage. A love crisis is a challenge to mobilize the best in yourself and grow.

EXERCISE

Place your focused attention—thoughts, feelings, and imagination—on each of the following for one minute:

- I can recall an especially happy and loving experience I've had.
- I remember how fortunate and blessed I really am.
- I like a lot of things about my love partner.
- My life is mostly wonderful.

Now, how do you feel?

LISTS

On my desk I have several lists:
TO DO:
TO CALL:
TO ORDER:
TO BUY:
TO CHECK:
TO REPAIR:

Why don't I ever make a list of:
good feelings to REMEMBER
special moments to CHERISH
things to be GRATEFUL for
people who have given *me* GIFTS
DAYS OF LOVE

PROBLEMS DON'T HAVE TO MAKE YOU MISERABLE

◆ To some people this idea may seem revolutionary, but problems don't have to make you unhappy! Life will always have its share of difficulties, in the midst of which you can choose to be satisfied and loving.

◆ The key is to take more responsibility—indeed, the opportunity— for developing your own happiness and well-being. You have the power to become the person you want to be.

◆ Make a plan, establish priorities. Don't set your goals too high. Favor making positive changes, rather than just focusing on the negative. Keep a chart or a self-improvement diary.

◆ Move one step at a time. You can't solve all your problems at once. Trying to do too much too soon is a sure way to meet failure and frustration. Balance patience with persistence.

◆ Enlist the support of family members and friends. Seek a self-help group. People going through similar changes together (losing weight, a fitness program, personal growth) can offer great support to one another.

◆ Recognize that plateaus will occur. Growth occurs in stages of rest and activity—sometimes one step backward for every two steps forward. Neither a body, a mind, nor a relationship change in a smooth, continuous fashion. Don't be discouraged; stay with your improvement plan. Plateaus and setbacks are natural to progress.

EXERCISE

What is a reasonable, major change in your life you would like to make? How might you go about this? Draw up a sensible plan; set yourself up to win. Monitor your progress with a chart or self-improvement diary. Join a self-help group.

THE ROSES IN MY GARDEN

The roses in my garden
are more beautiful,
more fragrant,
and give me more pleasure,
than any I can buy in a store.

And so it is with my children,
who are smarter than all others
and have my exquisite taste in art
and my great life-style.

Unless, of course,
it is the opposite,
and my roses are really runty,
and my children are not so terrific,
and my taste is unsure,
and my life-style is for the birds.

None of which
has to do with reality
but with the way
I feel today.

HAPPINESS IS LIKE A KISS

♦ No amount of striving is going to win you lasting happiness. No amount of manipulating, owning, or controlling is going to lead to fulfillment. The less able you are to experience inner pleasure, the more material symbols—a bigger house, faster car, more drugs—are sought to try to satisfy your thirst for it.

♦ There is an old saying, "Happiness is like a kiss. To get any good out of it, you have to give it to someone else!" Happiness is a by-product of being useful to others or devoted to a worthy cause.

♦ Aim high, let your highest principles guide your life, and you will find happiness on the way. Orienting your life to creative expression, the well-being of others, or the improvement of humankind, gives your pleasure significance.

♦ You become a lover of life not just by taking a philosophical stance, but through a passionate commitment to integrate your personal growth with social contribution. Once aware, the worst evil may be to remain passive. Everywhere, there are opportunities to make a difference.

♦ As your happiness expands, you learn a noble truth: The highest form of pleasure comes when you give yourself in love.

EXERCISE

What are three things you could do that would add greater meaning and purpose to your life?

THE SECRET OF HAPPINESS

Every day, have
something to do
or somewhere to go
every day have
someone to call
or someone to see
but most important
every day have
something to give
to someone

TWO HALVES
DON'T MAKE A WHOLE

♦ A mate or partner is sometimes selected in an attempt to achieve wholeness. This may lead to treating the other person like a part of you—an appendage, not a person in his own right. One person will then be threatened by his or her partner's growth. What is experienced by one as growth is perceived by the other with fear or envy.

♦ In a mature love one's individuality is not lost, but nurtured. Each partner experiences freedom, independence, and integrity. It's beautiful to need each other, but remember, wholeness comes mainly from within. Two halves make two halves; two whole loving persons can create a great relationship.

♦ It is easy, almost natural, to blame your love partner for your own problems and failures. People tend to unload personal frustrations on whomever is nearest and dearest. When you feel bored, moody, or frustrated, you may be expecting your love partner to magically boost your spirits.

♦ When you believe that you are responsible for your lover's distress, you feel guilty and worry that his or her frustration is somehow your fault. Taking unreasonable responsibility for your lover's moods and well-being gets in the way of his or her growing up.

EXERCISE

Do you feel a need to overprotect or save your love partner? Do you worry that your love partner will outgrow you? When your love partner is frustrated or unhappy, do you feel guilty?

THE BEST OF TIMES

It may not be a perfect time
but it's the best of times
when women can be strong
and not dependent
upon men
to earn a living

We're living in the best of times
when men can be emotional
and not dependent
upon women
to cook and clean and raise their children

We're living in the best of times
when all of us
are free to be whatever
we choose to be.

THERE IS MORE TO MARITAL READINESS THAN A BLOOD TEST

♦ There is more to marital readiness than a blood test! How lamentable that we spend so many years training for a career and yet prepare so little for marriage.

♦ Haste makes waste. A hasty courtship can sometimes lead to awful entanglements. Delaying marriage, by choice or because of financial or educational circumstances, is usually beneficial. The passage of time dispels a false infatuation, while it tempers and hones a true love and spiritual affinity.

♦ Trying to escape from an unhappy home into a marriage is often like jumping from the proverbial frying pan into the fire. Over 60 percent of teenage marriages end in divorce. The more mature you are at the time of marriage, the more durable will be your union.

♦ Be doubly sure before you sign on the dotted line. Have talks with yourself, your lover, friends, and family. Invite feedback from those you trust. Marriage is nothing to be impulsive about.

♦ Your choice of a mate might be very different after you've grown and experienced more and know better what you want. Complete your education, explore your talents, see the world. Unfold your latent potentialities, then consider marriage. Strength begets strength; fulfilled individuals make for a creative and powerful marriage.

♦ A healthy choice requires that you not decorate your beloved with illusory values. The heat of passion can color your senses and good judgment. But passion bubbles burst, giving rise to disappointment and frustration.

♦ Marriage is more than a honeymoon—it is a potential lifetime contract. Through sickness and health, for richer and for poorer, marriage requires devotion, a mature ability to commit.

EXERCISE

Have you and your love partner discussed money, domestic chores, childrearing, monogamy, family, values, and career goals?

GO AWAY A LITTLE CLOSER

She wants a commitment
he wants his options open
she's afraid to be used
he's afraid of dependency
she wants him to care for her
he wants her to want him
she's afraid of a lifetime
of loneliness
he's afraid of a lifetime
of responsibilities

for women, commitment comes too slowly
for men, it is too fast

STAND TOGETHER BUT NOT TOO NEAR

♦ The need for individual autonomy is not only compatible with a successful marriage, but can be a strong contributor. Some persons with highly developed individuality may need each other less, but paradoxically, feel free to love each other more. Neither partner is restricted by personal insecurities. They can share great closeness, yet can easily move apart.

♦ Give yourself the freedom to be apart. Some couples stifle romance with constant togetherness. Absence can make the heart grow fonder. You will have the excitement of discovering each other anew.

♦ Strive for a relationship of equals, each responsible for his or her own health and happiness, loved and encouraged by the other. Do "your thing," but don't impose it on your love partner. Love allows each partner to unfold in his or her own way.

♦ You cannot burden your lover with all your needs. The more self-sufficient you can be, the less pressure you put on the relationship. You will always have a need for professional self-esteem and close friends that no love relationship can replace.

♦ Love includes letting go when your partner needs freedom; holding your partner close when he or she needs care. It means wanting the best for your partner without feeling threatened by your partner's wins.

- Don't smother each other; no one can grow in the shade.
- Exclusive need not mean possessive.
- Structure need not mean rigid.
- Concern need not mean suffocation.
- Devotion need not mean servitude.

EXERCISE

Can you freely express your need for greater closeness as well as for more private time? Do you feel that you and your lover are equal partners? Do you think one of you has a better deal?

SEPARATIONS/REUNIONS

When we're together
for a long time
we feel connected
even take each other
for granted at times

When we're separated
for a while
we are disconnected
feeling cut off
even disoriented at times

When we are reunited again
we need to reconnect
we need a transition
from alone to coupled
we need time

MAKE KEY DECISIONS TOGETHER; TAKE EQUAL RESPONSIBILITY FOR THE RESULTS

♦ Love is embracing differences and discovering ways in which to build a common life-style, share decision making, and take equal responsibility for the results. Work together as partners without competing or putting the other person down. Make key choices together, fully listening to and learning from what your love partner has to say.

♦ As long as both partners are willing to keep on exploring their differences, all key decisions can be mutually resolved. The final decision is often a synthesis that was not even imagined before the exploration of options began.

EXERCISE

From the following list, select the area(s) in which you and your lover experience significant conflict and tension:

- finances
- childrearing
- extended family, in-laws, ex-spouses
- career versus home
- time management
- sex, quality intimacy
- life-style, personal habits

At a time when both of you are most relaxed, creatively brainstorm, looking for choices that will reduce stress and make for a happier life-style. For example, you may choose to go out to dinner one less evening per week and apply the savings toward a housekeeper. Or take turns having special time with your child, giving your spouse some leisure time for athletics, music, or hobbies.

COMPETITION

If I think
I am better than you
and you think
you are smarter than me
we will spend
a lot of time
trying to persuade
each other
of our particular
superiority

Time
we can spend better
discovering
each other

THE COUPLE THAT PLAYS TOGETHER STAYS TOGETHER

♦ All work and no play makes any love relationship dull. Marriage doesn't always have to be "grown up." You can increase your energy for problem-solving, challenges, and responsibilities by taking time out for fun and play.

♦ People put a lot of energy into things other than their relationship. With just a little extra care and enthusiasm, you can avoid getting locked into boring routines. Take turns creating an adventure day or weekend outing that would be memorable and exciting for both of you.

♦ Very often one person in the relationship does more to create romance and play than the other. If you've experienced this, and resent your partner for not trying harder to make things more interesting, communicate your desire without blame: "I'd love it if you would create a fun or adventuresome date for us next weekend."

♦ Have a party in your bedroom. You might cover the bed with rose petals or tie balloons to the bedpost. Dress up, dress down, or wear something unexpected. Serve a candlelight dinner with pillows on the bedroom floor.

♦ Give your imagination and creativity free rein. The two of you might go back in time to reenact your courtship and when you first made love. Or you might write your partner a poem or arrange your own bouquet of flowers.

♦ Play is vital for continuing to experience each other as lovers. If you treat your mate as "my old man," or "the little wife at home," you will be bored, and so will your partner. Creative fun and adventure help keep the magic of love alive.

EXERCISE

Write down three specific fun or adventuresome things you'll do with your love partner over the next month.

CELEBRATIONS

When you're the one
who starts something
I'm the one to continue it

like an argument

When I'm the one
who initiates
you're the one
to keep it going

like lovemaking

But whether we argue
or make love
we are always celebrating

life together

KEEP FAITH IN YOUR MATE'S LOVE FOR YOU EVEN WHEN FOR A TIME HE OR SHE DOES NOT

♦ A significant determining factor in the success of any relationship is the assumption that you can make love work. Love means sticking it out and solving problems that arise rather than running away. Commitment requires a willingness to risk being hurt and rejected, and at times feeling unloved.

♦ Trust that your partner loves you, even when his or her actions may indicate otherwise. Your faith can pierce through walls of hurt and fear, and help reconnect your mate to his or her love.

♦ Love assumes at all times that your partner is lovable and loving in his or her essence, and that any negative behavior, such as threats, screams, and sulks, is a response to pain and frustration and is a challenge to further understanding.

♦ To experience love more deeply you must be vulnerable to hurt—not dwelling on it, or paying excessive attention to it, but recognizing that some pain inevitably comes with love.

EXERCISE

In any relationship there will be occasions when one lover needs more from the other. Be sensitive to those times and respond with consideration and loving gestures. There is nothing more welcome when your love partner is having doubts or feeling down than your heartfelt understanding and a loving hug.

HOMECOMING

When he comes home
after a long trip
he wants her right away.
She wants to talk first.

He needs to reconnect
through his body
She needs to reconnect
by the sharing of feelings.

When he comes home
after a long trip
he's hot and quick.
She warms up slowly.

She usually accedes
but she does it for him.
If he would wait
and they could talk
even for just a few minutes

they would be doing it
for each other.

SUCCESS DOESN'T DEPEND ON HOW MANY TIMES YOU FALL BUT ON HOW MANY TIMES YOU GET BACK UP

♦ A major life disappointment can stimulate you to learn some of your greatest lessons of the heart. Find the courage to accept your loss and learn from it. You may discover that your disappointment really was the best thing that could have happened to you.

♦ When your plans don't work out as expected, you have two choices. Feel sorry for yourself, doubt your ability, and bemoan your bad luck. Or accept the loss, hold on to your self-confidence, and look for the opportunity hidden in your disappointment.

♦ Have faith in your ability to succeed at what you attempt, and to get back up if you fail. The greatest rewards of living come when you step out of the bounds of your ordinary existence and extend yourself beyond what you believe are your limits.

♦ Whenever life disappoints you, find something bigger than your problems to inspire and challenge you. Choose one of your bigger dreams and start making it a reality. You must be willing to risk failure many times before you become accomplished at anything.

EXERCISE

What have been three major disappointments you have suffered and what lessons of the heart did you learn? What have you dreamed of doing but have not done as yet for fear of disappointment or failure?

WHY NOT?

Sometimes confident
Sometimes scared
Sometimes in charge
Sometimes dependent
Sometimes tigress
Sometimes lamb
Sometimes Mother Goose
Sometimes Goldilocks
Wanting to be assertive
afraid of the consequences
Wanting to be feminine
afraid of the powerlessness
Wanting male prerogatives
afraid to compete for them
Wanting my cake
and to eat it, too.

Well, why not?

TRIALS AND TRIBULATIONS ARE TO MAKE, NOT BREAK YOU

♦ Anything you do becomes artistry if motivated by the passion for excellence and stamped with your personal style. It also makes any task more likely to succeed and satisfying.

♦ The torch of life has been passed to you; make it burn as brightly as possible. One such as you will never pass this way again. You are unique, one of a kind. Fulfill your talents to the utmost!

♦ Advance in the direction of your ideals. There is a strong likelihood for you to become what you imagine yourself to be. A life worth living is not one that is easy, but one that is fully lived.

♦ Do not aim to just maintain, but to surpass yourself. Spend your life on something that will outlast you. Have faith in your highest destiny.

EXERCISE

How would you like to be remembered after you die? What would you be willing to die for? What are the five greatest achievements of your life? Write your own obituary.

After

I will start enjoying life
after I get myself organized

I will exercise more
after I have updated my filing system

I will take a vacation
after I clean out the attic

I will buy myself some nice clothes
after I lose some weight

I will spend more time with my family
after I finish pasting the pictures in the photo albums

I will start enjoying life
after it's too late

BE TRUE TO WHAT INSPIRES YOU

♦ When you are inspired you are more likely to be loving. You feel free, spontaneous, alive, natural, powerful, and enthusiastic.

♦ Many of us live the first half of our adult lives postponing satisfaction and the last half with regrets. Fulfillment seems always to be just over the next hill. You may be waiting for someone to make you happy and resenting that no one does.

♦ When you strive to do your best you stop worrying about how you compare with others. You are more likely to appreciate your own goodness and the goodness of others, and to enjoy being acknowledged not just for what you do but for who you are. The root meaning of *competition* is "to pursue together in excellence."

♦ Be your own person with distinct interests, ideas, values, and preferences. The more freely you express your individuality, the more satisfaction you'll get, the more passion and joy you'll experience with your love partner. Your happiness lies in discovering your own right way.

♦ Learn from your love partner. The point is not to decide whose beliefs and values are "right," but rather to understand and respect the reasons each of you has for believing as you do. Discover and support what inspires your love partner.

EXERCISE

How well do you live up to your moral, spiritual, and ethical values? What three things have you done that you are most ashamed of? What three ethical choices have you made that you are most proud of?

THE IMPORTANT PEOPLE

I used to watch
the important people having lunch
and wished I could eat
with them

I used to wonder
what the important people said
and wished I could talk
to them

I wanted to know
where the important people went
and wished I could go
with them

I tried to guess
what the important people did
and wished I could do it
with them

And now that I have lunch with them
and talk to them and go with them
I know that they look important
only from a distance

The important people
are no different from the people
who sat with me
when I used to watch
the important people
having lunch

LOVE IS BEST WITHOUT STRINGS ATTACHED; NO "IFS" OR "BUTS"

♦ When you say to your loved one, "I love you, but . . . ," you actually make a coercive statement which implies, "I won't love you unless you agree to do what I say."

♦ Love is best given without strings—no "ifs" or "buts." Love can say "no" when discipline or firmness is needed, but seeks to do so in a "yes" fashion, conveying security and acceptance.

♦ In a love relationship, each person seeks to promote the uniqueness and individuality of the other. The person is loved as he or she is, not for what he or she is expected to be. To give up what you want or value under pressure is to give up a sense of yourself.

♦ You won't enjoy saying "yes" to your partner, unless you also feel the freedom to say "no." You can give freely to your love partner, if you know you can say "no" without being punished. When you are not engaged in a power struggle, you can give with great pleasure rather than out of fear, duty, or guilt.

EXERCISE

Fill in five responses to the statement, "The ways I've attached strings to my love for you are . . ." What do you need to do to remove each of these strings, to be able to give of your love more freely?

HE/SHE

1. He brags about her looks
   She brags about his job

2. He thinks she's cute
   She thinks he's strong

3. He wants her to look pretty
   She wants him to sound intelligent

4. He is proud of her running the house well
   She is proud of his position at work

5. He repairs
   She mends

6. He barbecues
   She cooks

7. He likes her deference
   She likes his dominance

8. He admires her knowledge of the arts
   She admires his knowledge of politics

9. He has the right answers
   She has the right questions

10. He couldn't manage without her
    She couldn't manage without him

LOVE SECRET #56

DO WHAT YOU LOVE;
LOVE WHAT YOU DO

♦ It is very important to have a clear vision of possibilities, a realistic model of loving human beings in a happy and healthy marriage and family.

♦ Unfortunately, you may not have been exposed to a fully loving person in your family. During adolescence, you may have chosen a movie star, athlete, or rock singer as a role model. Rarely is a teen idol chosen for qualities of the heart.

♦ The ideal to be sought and emulated too often becomes the celebrity, the power of fame and money, instead of outstanding qualities of heart and mind. Culturally and individually we must be more careful whom we hold up for admiration and recognition, for especially in our formative years, we learn a great deal from modeling.

♦ Our culture is in need of a superior vision of our human capacity; the hero, the healer, the true leader, have fallen by the wayside. We must expose ourselves and our youth to the best of our species— the loving, creative, and dedicated person, though he or she is not a headliner.

♦ We, in the chain of humanity, have been taught that we are as weak as our weakest link. This is but half the truth—we are also as strong as our strongest link. Find loving models and emulate those qualities you admire most. Seek out and learn from those who love best.

EXERCISE

Who are the three people in history you admire most? Why?

What three people in your past had the most influence on your values and thinking? How?

Who are the most loving people in your life right now? Describe examples of their specific loving actions you most admire.

MODELS

My female model
is my mother
a traditional
non-professional
woman at home
with high standards
on how to run a house

My male models
are the men in the office
working sixty hours a week
because they have
wives like my mother
taking care of everything

If I'm like the men
I have no time
for anything except
work
evening meetings
and out-of-town business

If I'm like my mother
I have no time
for anything except
keeping the house spotless
having hot meals on time
and chauffeuring the children

The world needs new models.
We must be these models.

FRIENDSHIP IS ESSENTIAL TO LOVE

♦ It is a great joy—indeed, essential—to have a marriage partner whom you can utterly trust with the deepest murmurings of your soul. One who knows the best and the worst of you and yet loves you through and through; a friend as well as a lover.

♦ Some believe that being a good friend and being a spouse or lover are mutually exclusive, if not contradictory. This is just not so. Friendship is an important ingredient to a deep and lasting love relationship.

♦ During infatuation and early romance there is a tendency to focus on the beloved to the exclusion of your friends. This is a mistake. Don't let your close friendships disappear.

♦ Strong friendships are an important support to you and your love relationship. Friends lend encouragement during difficult times, as well as celebrate your good fortune.

♦ Honor thy friendships. "Do not," as the ancient Chinese admonish, "remove a fly from a friend's forehead with a hatchet." Use an ostrich feather instead. Close friends are a present; you get the friends and loved ones you deserve.

EXERCISE

Make a list of five ways that you could be a better friend to your love partner. List five ways in which you could be a better friend to yourself.

BEST FRIENDS

I have some friends I never see
who live thousands of miles away
we were best friends in college
or when our children were small

Now we call each other only
when we have good news
or when we're unhappy
or just need to reconnect

Neither the distance nor the years
seem to matter
we can start right up
where we left off

When there is no other way
good friends should be heard
if they can't be seen.

YOU AND YOUR PARTNER MAY NOT BE ALIKE IN YOUR TOLERANCE OR DESIRE FOR INTIMACY

♦ Love partners are not alike in their tolerance or desire for intimacy. While almost everyone could use more intimacy, people have different paces, styles, and comfort zones that must be respected. It is not inviting or intimate to demand intimacy!

♦ You may reach a new ability to be open and share yourself only to encounter resistance from your lover. Even if your lover is uncooperative at first, the more self-disclosing you are, the more likely he or she will gradually open. Talk from your heart and soon your love partner will follow you in his or her own way.

♦ Why is the fear of intimacy so widespread? The primary reason is that most people were exposed to unhealthy emotional habits from early childhood. Since they didn't see their parents as models for intimate conversation, they never learned its value, much less how to do it.

♦ There is no permanent victory in love; problems and challenges always arise. Growth in an intimate relationship is never in a straight, upward line. More often it takes an irregular path. When you feel yourselves starting to grow too far apart, it's time to reconnect.

EXERCISE

What "heart blocks" or fears of intimacy do you harbor? Do you ever "demand" intimacy? What is the result?

FEELING CLOSE

I like it best
when we can
be together
not being entertaining
not making conversation
not talking at all

silently intimate.

A CRISIS IS AN OPPORTUNITY FOR LOVE TO GROW

♦ In a long-term relationship there are times when love partners are inconsiderate, hurt each other's feelings, or let each other down. If these occasions are prolonged and severe, a crisis may result.

♦ A crisis in your love relationship can allow you to transform a destructive problem into a challenging opportunity for intense communication, greater commitment, more mutual respect, and ultimately, deeper love.

♦ You both must ask yourselves what you can do to make the relationship better. If both of you take 100 percent responsibility for creating the crisis, then effective dialogue and a commitment to change become possible.

♦ There is a fine line between communicating hurt feelings and destructively dumping, berating, and making your love partner wrong. It is not valuable to indulge in demeaning invectives such as, "You're a liar," "You never do anything right," or "I told you so!" Be specific about exactly what behavior or incident upset you and the feelings it generated in you.

♦ Real love begins when you are able to see the flaws and weaknesses in your partner and love him or her.

EXERCISE

In an emotional crisis you must resolve your anger, hurt, and sadness for love to grow.

> ANGER. Express your fury and resentment: "I'm fed up with . . ."; "I resent that . . ."; "I hate it when . . ."
>
> HURT. Express your disappointment and pain: "It hurts me when . . ."; "I feel insecure about . . ."
>
> SADNESS. Express your remorse and regret: "I'm sorry that . . ."; "I feel sad that . . ."
>
> LOVE. Express your care and understanding: "I forgive you for . . ."; "I forgive myself for . . ."; "I understand that . . ."; "What I have learned is . . ."; "I love you for . . ."

HIS SIDE

Yesterday it was:
"you're wonderful
you're handsome
you're so bright
you're the greatest lover
I'm so glad I'm married
    to you"

and I could do no wrong

Today it is:
"why don't you talk to
    me
you never listen
I need more money
not tonight, I have a
    headache"

and I can do no right

How did I get from
    adored husband
to bastard?

HER SIDE

Yesterday it was:
"my darling, my one
    and only
I will love you forever
I will always take care
    of you
you're my reason for
    living
I adore you"

and I could do no wrong

Today it is:
"get off my back
take care of it yourself
stop spending so much
I won't discuss it"

and I can do no right

How did I get from
    adored wife
to bitch?

CULTIVATE AN
ATTITUDE OF GRATITUDE

♦ Many people seem to believe that love is supposed to grow on its own without help from the two people involved. They get into the habit of forgetting to say "Thank you," "You look lovely," "That was beautiful," "I appreciate what you did for me," "You make me feel great when you do that," and so on. Gratitude is necessary for the growth of love!

♦ There is no need for a gushing sentimentality or saccharine flattery. The goal is to be able to express appreciation and positive regard, freely and appropriately. Developing your capacity to love and be loved is just like developing a musical talent or sports skill. The more you practice, the stronger, more confident, and more graceful you become.

♦ When you are feeling unappreciated, instead of complaining, "You never give me credit for how hard I work to provide a home and life-style you enjoy," try rephrasing your request with love: "Sweetheart, I've had a rough day, and when you get time, I need some hugs and understanding."

♦ If you or your lover are hurting, nothing may be more healing than a silent embrace.

> A huggle is
> a snuggle plus
> a cuddle with
> a hug

♦ At least one huggle a day helps keep the marriage counselor away.

EXERCISE

Share a huggle a day with your love partner.

ONE MOMENT

One moment
on a sofa
we are
two strangers

We can talk about
the latest movie
the newest novel
or the last trip

One moment
on a sofa
can be nothing

OR

We can talk about
your worries
my family
our hopes

And in one moment
on a sofa
each can touch
the other's life

CREATE A LOVE NEST

♦ Consider setting aside a separate room or part of a bedroom as a love nest. Create a special place for just the two of you. Let the room be expressive of each of your styles and tastes. Here are a few suggestions:

- thick, soft carpet, or throw rugs to comfortably make love upon
- cushions—big and small, soft and firm
- drapes to maximize privacy but which allow in natural light
- your favorite colors
- illumination that is soft and warm
- sandalwood or rose incense—the long-burning kind
- fresh flowers or plants
- soft and easy love songs
- your favorite art
- toys and treasures

♦ Many couples get so caught up in their everyday lives—career, finances, children—that they stop putting energy into their relationship without even realizing it. Soon the relationship suffers. Making your love sanctuary more beautiful and comfortable is one way to enliven and make special your intimacy.

EXERCISE

What changes or additions might you make to create a love nest?

KINKY SEX

Some do it hanging from chandeliers
others enjoy group sex

Some do it with animals
others like it with drugs

Some do it in strange positions
others search for exotic settings

Some do it in public places
others prefer it alone

I like to hug and kiss
and talk a lot
about our thoughts and feelings

and do it in the comfort of our bed
when the house is quiet
and the children asleep

and then take time
to hug and kiss
and mostly talk a lot

HEARTFELT MASSAGE

♦ Apart from sexual desire, each of us has a deep need for tenderness, caressing, and touch. You can derive as much pleasure from giving a massage as receiving one. What you will need is a warm, quiet setting; soft lighting; scented oil; a firm mattress; a soft pillow, and soothing music or silence (please, take the phone off the hook).

♦ Touch continuously in a regular, easy rhythm. Use the full surface of your hands. Keep your fingers together. Develop your personal style, but always stay smooth and symmetrical. Take plenty of time—don't rush.

♦ There are different strokes—circling, pressing, kneading, rotating, shaking, lifting, pulling—for different folks. Ask your partner to describe what he or she enjoys.

♦ Don't neglect any body parts. The head, hands, legs, and feet are all too often neglected. A soft hairbrush, shampooing the scalp, a rolling pin on the back and legs, a vibrator (or two, one in each hand), and an alcohol rub can add special and delightful effects.

♦ An atmosphere of safety and trust is essential. Never criticize your partner for being "uptight," tense, or guarded. The tension will gradually fade. The body is a temple, the container of your loved one's soul.

EXERCISE

Give a massage this week to someone you love.

Ask for a massage this week from someone you love.

Caution: Don't have great expectations and set yourself up for disappointment. Appreciate whatever your lover is able to give you.

THE REAL DIFFERENCE
BETWEEN MEN AND WOMEN

He likes to be touched
anytime
anywhere
he always likes to be touched
caressed
fondled
he's always ready
always eager

Sometimes she doesn't want
to be touched
hugged, yes
touched, no

He doesn't understand
that sometimes her body
needs to be left alone
but, so that he shouldn't feel rejected
she lets him touch her anyway
reluctantly

And then he says
"see, you liked it"
and there are times
that she does
and times
that she doesn't

SLOW DOWN;
SAVOR YOUR LOVER

◆ Slow motion builds passion; this is the single most important "sexual exercise." An orchestra does not open with a crescendo, and you can't make a symphony out of lovemaking if you rush to climax. Slowing down allows you to tune into your own and your partner's feelings.

◆ Lovemaking doesn't mean you must immediately fondle each other's genitals. Try a feather-light stroking with your fingertips. Or light kisses on the nape of the neck, between the breasts, along the stomach and inner thighs. Use your imagination and enjoy.

◆ Communicate with sensitivity what you find most pleasurable and erotic, such as, "I like it when you . . ."; "It turns me on when you let me . . ."; "I'd prefer if you would . . ." Expressing your feelings increases love and trust and lessens pressure and anxiety.

◆ Give yourself and your partner permission to enjoy. No need to pretend, perform, or feign some imagined "ideal." Good sex is what's good for you and your partner. Trying to measure how much, how many, or how often, inhibits pleasure.

◆ Love can be felt spiritually and physically; one does not rule out the other. Instead of a mechanical preoccupation with foreplay and climax, lovemaking can become a graceful, ecstatic merging.

EXERCISE

What three things might you do in your love play if you were sure no one would be hurt or laugh at you?

MUSIC

As I lie next to you
I am your violin
all smooth curves
waiting to be played upon

as you lie next to me
you are my bow
straight and thin
rigidly poised
in expectation

slowly you fine-tune my body
listening for the different sounds
our music makes
as your bow glides
over my body

at first tentatively
testing the chords
then gently
plucking at the strings

until the soft humming
becomes a duet
then a string ensemble
some brass joins in
finally the full orchestra
explodes in a symphony
of cymbals and drums

the applause is silent

PUT LOVE FIRST TO MAKE PASSION LAST

♦ Love is the foundation for sex, not sex the foundation for love. The sexual drive, in its deepest and most profound sense, has the force of universal love behind it. The sex drive seeks not just sensory gratification but union.

♦ Sex "ups the ante" in the early phases of a relationship, making it more likely to become bonded. Sexual pleasures may be so overshadowing that it becomes difficult to discern whether you really like each other or get along!

♦ The once cherished dogmas of "liberated sex"—erotic pleasure without consequence, multiple partners without jealousy, recreation without creation—have proven false. "Liberated sex" has bred sexual exploitation, performance fears, manipulation, disease, unwanted pregnancies, boredom, and spiritual malaise.

♦ Monogamy, when freely chosen, becomes a spiritual quest. There is no external place to go; you must go to the core of love within yourself and your partner.

♦ When you and your love partner can share your passion without fear, and with patience, commitment, and trust, emotional sharing can generate a limitless flow of sexual energy.

EXERCISE

Make a list beginning with the statement, "The ways I've been blocking love in my life are . . ." Here are some examples:

- By getting angry and demanding sex.
- By working too hard, and then using sex to reduce stress rather than express love.
- By trying so hard to make my partner have an orgasm that I stop feeling tender or caring.

FOREPLAY

It starts in the morning
when I wake up
as you hold me
and ask me how I slept.

It starts at breakfast
when you tell me
what you'll be doing at work
and where you can be reached.

It's how sweetly you kiss me
when you leave
and it continues during the day
when you call just to say hello.

It's when you come home
and hug me
and tell me you've missed me
and ask me about my day.

It goes on during dinner
when we listen to each other
and you hold my hand
as we share our thoughts.

And when we finally go to bed
I am ready to make love.

INTIMATE SEX TALKS

♦ Be willing to share your deeper sexual fears and feelings with your love partner. For example, "I worry about sexually pleasing you"; "I get frustrated trying to seduce or turn you on"; "When it comes to sex, I sometimes feel you just want to 'get right to it' and don't enjoy cuddling or getting me aroused."

♦ The more open, honest, and specific you are, the more receptive you will be to learning about each other's sexuality while discovering greater intimacy: "What I need to let you know about my sexual needs is . . ."; "You could excite me sexually by . . ."; "I would feel less pressured if . . ."; "Some of the ways we could be more sexually intimate without intercourse are . . ."

♦ You and your love partner can create great freedom by establishing a bond of trust that alleviates the pressure and fear of judgment, rejection, and performance. Being together in a fully present and intimate way opens the channel of communication to allow for full disclosure of emotions and desires.

♦ Sex can be a routine act of fulfilling desire, in which case boredom is inevitable, or it can be a window of discovery for you and your love partner with a depth of passion to last a lifetime.

EXERCISE

Take turns sharing with one or two of the following sex talks:

- "The best thing about our sex life is . . ."
- "We would improve our experience of sex by . . ."
- "I feel most sexually turned on to you when . . ."
- "What I would like to add to our sexual and physical intimacy is . . ."
- "The way I would most like to be touched is . . ."

SEXUAL TENSIONS

Looking into
each other's eyes

hoping the other
will initiate
what both want

but neither daring
to make the first move

IF YOU'RE BORED, MAYBE YOU'VE LET YOURSELF BECOME BORING

♦ Take responsibility for tuning in to the pleasure of your own body, including orgasm. Get to know your sexuality; show your partner what turns you on. The better you know your own body, the more sexual joy you will have to share.

♦ Whatever you find yourselves doing in the flow of sexual love-making is right and beautiful. There can be much pleasure in being passively used, in giving service, in vigorously rubbing, squeezing, or biting. Wrestle, lick, suck; do whatever is pleasurable, as long as it is kept within mutually acceptable limits.

♦ Sex can be a barometer of intimacy in a long-term relationship. When sex goes flat and remains boring, often the relationship is on its way to trouble.

♦ In the beginning of a relationship, partners excite each other primarily by revealing and sharing their bodies. In a maturing sexual relationship, partners can discover an even greater source of sexual excitement by revealing their emotional selves and communicating heart-to-heart in sexual play.

EXERCISE

What behavior in you would you find boring if you were your partner? You and your love partner should each separately complete the statements below in writing and then exchange your answers afterward:

- "A sexual delight I would like to indulge in with you is . . ."
- "You could excite me sexually by . . ."
- "I would like to excite you sexually by . . ."
- "A sexual fantasy I would like to act out with you is . . ."

MISSED CONNECTIONS

When he wants it

she doesn't

When she's ready

he can't

YOUR SEXUAL FULFILLMENT IS PRIMARILY UP TO YOU, NOT YOUR LOVE PARTNER

◆ Sexual functioning requires a relatively rested and relaxed state of mind and body. A temporary bout of premature ejaculation, impotence, or difficulty with orgasm may be the result of fatigue, worries, overeating, or a recent emotional loss. These generally will go away on their own. Some ebb and flow in sexual responsiveness is natural.

◆ To enjoy sex depends partially on maintaining some simple, healthful habits: stay well rested, eat lightly, drink in moderation, practice good hygiene, and exercise regularly.

◆ Sexual difficulties may result from negative feelings of fear, shame, or anger. These emotions can inhibit spontaneous abandon and sexual responsiveness.

◆ Some people turn to alcohol in an attempt to cope with fear, shame, or anger. A small amount of alcohol may temporarily reduce anxiety, but overall, alcohol has a depressant effect upon sexuality. Chronic alcohol abuse may lead to impotence or orgasmic incompetence.

◆ Another small but significant cause of sexual dysfunction is organic impairment. Some of the typical illnesses that can disrupt sexual functioning are diabetes, multiple sclerosis, and thyroid dysfunction. Your doctor can provide a thorough medical exam.

EXERCISE

To help recognize and release inhibitions to your sexual pleasure, explore the following:

- "Three sexual fears I have are . . ."
- "Sexual thoughts I feel guilty about are . . ."
- "My parents gave me the impression sex was . . ."
- "The experiences I had that led me to associate sex with shame were . . ."

YOU TURN ME ON

You turn me on
not only by what you say
or how you touch me
but by just being you

I look at you
and get turned on
the way you stand
or move or talk

The way you think
the way you look at me
the way you are
turns me on

ENJOY X-RATED FANTASY

♦ Many people are troubled by guilt feelings caused by sexual fantasies. It is quite natural to have fantasies—often outrageous ones, at that. By any criteria or classification, quite normal people report fantasies of group sex, homosexuality, and extramarital affairs. Sexual fantasies are just that; they require neither action nor guilt.

♦ Give yourself permission to have fantasies. If you have a willing partner you might act them out (except for those that are truly offensive, violent, or dangerous). Anything goes as long as love prevails: touch, tongue, tickle; silk, satin, lace; the kitchen table or the couch.

♦ No matter how committed you are to your love partner, monogamy of the mind is not only difficult, it is probably impossible. Fantasy is a powerful stimulus to sexual pleasure.

♦ One caution: It is important to create an intimate and trusting atmosphere for sharing sexual fantasies. Disclosing your fantasies without warning, to arouse jealousy or hostility, can bring devastating results. Sexual fantasies are normal, but there is no need to offend your love partner.

EXERCISE

Allow yourself the freedom to act out a safe fantasy, giving your imagination and creativity free rein. Take turns or else create a fantasy together. Here are some examples:

- The two of you go back to when you were dating and the first time you made love.
- You imagine playing the courtesan and the conqueror; you take turns being at each other's beck and call.
- You each write an erotic fantasy and read it to the other.

FANTASIES

She is the slave of an Arab sheik
who makes wild love to her
in his desert tent

She is a go-go girl
dancing nude
in a Las Vegas bar

She's a prim spinster
carried off
by some primitive man

She's a porn movie queen
performing in front of
a large camera crew

Her secret fantasies
may be exciting
but if any of them
really happened
they would become
terrible nightmares

DIVINE SEX

♦ The ancient practice of tantra makes sex not just a biological function, but a divine and sacred ritual. It is for soul mates in search of a supreme love experience, and not an exotic mechanical procedure.

♦ Tantra is for married or very intimate partners to practice, after meditation or just before retiring. The whole experience takes at least an hour; allow for total privacy and no sense of rushing.

♦ Sexual excitement builds up in waves and settles down; the slower the buildup the better. Sexual intercourse is enjoyed with ease, rapport, and abandon. Sexual movements are subtle, spontaneous, and from the inside. There is no urgency to orgasm.

♦ In the classic tantra position, the woman settles into the lap of her lover, each with arms encircling the other. But, please, comfort is essential, so any sexual position can be enjoyed.

♦ Each partner can experience fully the pleasure of the other. Ejaculation and orgasm may or may not be desired. Every atom of the body is overwhelmed with ecstasy, rapture, and grandeur.

EXERCISE

The goal of tantra is to enjoy a slow buildup of sexual energy and cosmic union, not a quick orgasm. Several seconds prior to ejaculation, the male experiences pleasurable contractions. If he stops thrusting when he feels them, he can postpone ejaculation. When you stop, don't get lost in fantasy. Breathe deeply and relax. The pressure for orgasm will lessen. After a few minutes, slow pelvic thrusting can be resumed. The result is a wonderful buildup of intimacy and pleasure. The joy is in subtly experiencing together your love and sexual energy; you may or may not choose, or even care, to have an orgasm.

KISSES

When you kiss me
I feel expanded
your love
fills me with
something tangible
like surges
of energy

When you kiss me
it makes me stronger
yet I feel weak
at the same time
hormones releasing chemicals
exchanging electrical charges
with you

MEDITATING OPENS THE HEART

♦ When made a regular part of your daily routine, meditation increases your capacity for love and enjoyment. Anxiety, tension, and irritability are reduced; doubts and insecurities fade.

♦ Medical research confirms that in meditation you experience a state of very deep rest, marked by decreased heart rate, oxygen consumption, muscle tension, and blood pressure. Increased coherence of brain-wave activity contributes to mental clarity and lasting emotional ease.

♦ When relaxation and quiet pleasure are the basic bond in a relationship, the likelihood of deepening love and emotional rewards is great. Intimacy, the most profound of interpersonal human pleasures, grows in an atmosphere of peace.

♦ The Transcendental Meditation (TM) technique is the most scientifically researched and reliable method you can practice. It is easy, effortless, and highly enjoyable. Call your local TM center to learn more about how you can learn as an individual or couple.

EXERCISE

Meditating regularly opens your heart and allows you to see your partner anew. To counteract taking your love partner for granted today, choose to see him or her as a total stranger. Assume your lover has had a personality transformation and looks familiar, but you don't know him or her. See your partner with new eyes and renewed interest. How many new things can you discover about your partner?

MEDITATION

I run around
all day
fretting about
what others say
what others need
what others think

It's only when
I take the time
to stop awhile
and go inward
that I find out
what I say
what I need
what I think

It's only when
I take the time
to stop awhile
that I know
what you say
what you need
what you think

It's only when I know me
that I can know you

SPIRITUAL VALUES

♦ Values are your own personal, private beliefs about what is most important to you. Values determine what you will turn away from and what you will move toward.

♦ Higher values give meaning and purpose to your relationship. You and your partner have come together not only for the benefit of one another but for everyone.

♦ Shared spiritual values are the basis for a lasting, fulfilling relationship. You put trust and faith in each other and in God (life, nature, or a higher power).

EXERCISE

What matters most to you and your partner in an intimate relationship? You and your partner should each rank the values listed below in order of importance:

commitment	love	communication
fun	adventure	physical attraction
service	respect	passion
honesty	lifestyle	children
family	religion	support

Use your lists to explore with one another:

What is most important to you about your love relationship?
What values do you appreciate most in your partner?
What values do you want to be most appreciated for?
What goals and beliefs give meaning to your life?

HANDS

My right hand is being held
by someone who knows more than I,
and I am learning.
My left hand is being held
by someone who knows less than I,
and I am teaching.

Both my hands need thus be held
for me to be.

WHAT YOU DON'T GIVE, YOU LOSE

♦ As your love develops, your appreciation of your interdependence with every other human being grows as well. The more love you feel, the more love you want to share. Personal growth and social contribution become woven into one strand.

♦ You come to appreciate that life is one; an outpouring of love flows through you toward your fellow human beings and all creation. Love becomes a deeper experience of unity amid diversity; the unfolding mystery and beauty of life.

♦ To the extent you put *Love Secrets for a Lasting Relationship* to use, you will break through old barriers and past resistances to new levels of emotional strength and honest communication. You will overcome old, negative habits and experience more love and pleasure.

♦ You will become more attuned to your loved ones and discover your power to create the life you want. With these tools, your perspective is likely to grow from "me" to "we," and you are likely to become more concerned about making the rest of the world a better place.

♦ There is today a rising spirituality, sometimes imperceptible, but becoming increasingly more evident: respect for the sacredness of every person, species, and culture; greater appreciation for nature and the universe. Follow your bliss and integrity; let the spirit of love work through you.

EXERCISE

Put your compassion for others into action. Take a few hours out of your busy schedule to volunteer your time and energy for a worthy cause. For example, serve food to the homeless, teach someone to read, or help clean up the environment.

Follow Your Heart

Go where the heart
longs to go
Don't pay attention to the feet
who want to stay rooted

Go where the mind
wants to explore
Don't worry about the hands
who still want to hold on

Go where your gut
is fearful to go
Don't let your body
sit in one place

Go where your heart
longs to go

DEAR READER,

I would like to hear from you. What are your love secrets? What lessons of the heart have you discovered to make love last? What love exercises do you practice that make a difference in the quality of your marriage and family life? I would appreciate your sharing with me the love secrets you have learned.

Thank you.

Best,
Harold

For further information regarding Harold H. Bloomfield, M.D.'s personal appearances and seminars, and to order audiotape and video products as supplements to *Love Secrets for a Lasting Relationship*, please call or send a self-addressed envelope to:

HAROLD H. BLOOMFIELD, M.D.
1011 Camino Del Mar
Del Mar, California 92014
(619) 481-7102

OTHER BOOKS YOU MAY WISH TO CONSULT

Bloomfield, Harold H., with Leonard Felder. *Making Peace With Your Parents*. New York: Random House, 1983.

Bloomfield, Harold H., with Leonard Felder. *Making Peace With Yourself* (formerly titled *The Achilles Syndrome*). New York: Random House, 1985.

Bloomfield, Harold H., and Robert B. Kory. *Inner Joy*. New York: Wyden, 1980.

Bloomfield, Harold H., and Sirah Vettese, with Robert B. Kory. *Lifemates*. New York: New American Library, 1989.

Colgrove, Melba, Harold H. Bloomfield, and Peter McWilliams. *How to Survive the Loss of a Love*. New York: Bantam, 1977.

Josefowitz, Natasha. *Is This Where I Was Going?* New York: Warner, 1983.

Josefowitz, Natasha. *Natasha's Words for Lovers*. New York: Warner, 1986.

Lazarus, Arnold. *Marital Myths*. San Luis Obispo: Impact Publishers, 1985.

Rogers, Carl. *Becoming Partners*. New York: Delacorte Press, 1973.

Index of Love Secrets

\# 1 • Love Is Not Enough   2

\# 2 • You May Be Attracted to Characteristics in a Love Partner You Later Become Repelled By   4

\# 3 • Love Is Not a License to Seek to Change or Control Your Partner   6

\# 4 • What You Resist, Persists; What You Accept, Lightens   8

\# 5 • Never Assume You Know What Your Partner Is "Really" Thinking or Feeling; Lovers Are Not Mind Readers   10

\# 6 • Love Guarantees Some Hurt, Anger, and Frustration; It Goes with the Territory   12

\# 7 • Listen to Your Love Partner's Criticism Without Interrupting, Judging, or Contradicting   14

\# 8 • No One Gets 100 Percent Approval   16

\# 9 • When It Comes to Feelings, No One Is Wrong   18

\# 10 • Safety and Trust Are More Important Than Love   20

\# 11 • Respect Is Essential to Love; Noticing with Attention   22

\# 12 • Blaming and Complaining Don't Work   24

\# 13 • Problems Are Equally Created   26

\# 14 • There Is Such a Thing as a Good Argument   28

\# 15 • When You Make an Emotional Mistake (Everybody Does), Acknowledge It and Apologize   30

\# 16 • Favor the Positive   32

\# 17 • Get Unstuck and Lighten Up   34

\# 18 • Take Time for Yourself and You'll Have More Love to Give Your Partner   36

\# 19 • You Deserve Appreciation but Sometimes You Must Ask for It   38

\# 20 • A Love Relationship Built on Excitement Alone Is Doomed to Failure   40

\# 21 • Jealousy Is Sometimes the Surest Way to Get Rid of the Very Person You Are Afraid of Losing   42

\# 22 • Forgive Yourself for Not Being Perfect   44

\# 23 • No Pain, No Gain 46

\# 24 • A Broken Heart Requires as Much Care as a Broken Leg 48

\# 25 • Love's Great Dampener Is Chronic Fatigue 50

\# 26 • Depression Impairs the Ability to Love and Be Loved and Is Too Often Overlooked 52

\# 27 • Your Unfinished Business with Parents Affects Your Adult Love Life 54

\# 28 • You May Experience with Your Love Partner the Hurt, Fear, and Anger You Felt as a Child 56

\# 29 • What You Believe to Be So, Becomes So; You Get the Love Relationship You Think You Deserve 58

\# 30 • Forgiving Your Love Partner Primarily Benefits You 60

\# 31 • Water Your Family Roots to Enjoy Love's Fruits 62

\# 32 • Know When to Get Help 64

\# 33 • A Loving Attitude Is Contagious 66

\# 34 • No One Can Make You Feel Inferior Without Your Consent 68

\# 35 • Trust Your Inner Voice 70

\# 36 • No Matter How Good or Committed Your Love Relationship, You Will Always Be "Single" 72

\# 37 • Your Happiness Is Primarily Up to You, Not Your Love Partner 74

\# 38 • There Is No Barrier to Feeling Attractive, Only Your Belief 76

\# 39 • Just as Dissatisfaction with Yourself Is Contagious, So Is Enthusiasm 78

\# 40 • Fitness Gives You Energy for Loving Fully 80

\# 41 • Appreciate Yourself as You Are as a Basis for Change 82

\# 42 • All Growth Is the Integration of Seemingly Opposite Values 84

\# 43 • What You Place Attention on Grows Stronger 86

\# 44 • Problems Don't Have to Make You Miserable 88

\# 45 • Happiness Is Like a Kiss 90

\# 46 • Two Halves Don't Make a Whole 92

\# 47 • There Is More to Marital Readiness Than a Blood Test 94

\# 48 • Stand Together but Not Too Near 96

\# 49 • Make Key Decisions Together; Take Equal Responsibility for the Results 98

Index of Poems

After, 107
Are You More If I'm Less?, 73
Ask Me, Don't Tell Me, 15
Before and After, 13
Best Friends, 115
Best of Times, The, 93
Blues, The, 53
Bodies, 79
Celebrations, 101
Competition, 99
Conundrums, 9
Dealing with Her Success, 23
Disappointment, 41
Empowerment, 85
Exercise, 81
Extramarital Affair, 43
False Expectations, 11
Families, 63
Fantasies, 137
Fantasy at a Party, 7
Feeling Close, 117
Follow Your Heart, 145
Food, 81
Foreplay, 129
Go Away a Little Closer, 95
Hands, 143
He/She, 111
Her Side, 119
His Side, 119
Homecoming, 103
I Did It Again, 25
I Don't Love Him Anymore, 29
I Sound Just Like My Mother, 55
I Think You're Wonderful, 67
I'm Always Tired, 51
I'm Not OK, You're Not OK, but That's OK, 21
Important People, The, 109
Key to Happiness?, The, 65
Kinky Sex, 123

Kisses, 139
Lies?, 31
Lists, 87
Lose/Win, 47
Lost and Found, 49
Love Ache, 3
Love Secrets, 1
Meditation, 141
Meeting, 5
Missed Connections, 133
Models, 113
Moving Beyond, 59
Music, 127
Needed: Body Parts, 57
Needed: Mutual Support, 27
No Exit, 37
Not Halloween, 71
OK Person Seal of Approval, The, 83
One Moment, 121
Priorities, 33
Real Difference Between Men and Women, The, 125
Remorse and Regret, 45
Roses in My Garden, The, 89
Secret of Happiness, The, 91
Separations/Reunions, 97
Sexual Tensions, 131
Tomorrow I Will Change, 75
Toys Are Us, 35
Trust, 15
Truth, The, 17
Unafraid, 69
When I'm Fully in Charge of Me, 19
Whole Is More Than the Sum of Its Parts, The, 39
Why Not?, 105
Wrong Century, 77
You Hurt Me, 61
You Turn Me On, 135

\# 50 • THE COUPLE THAT PLAYS TOGETHER STAYS TOGETHER 100

\# 51 • KEEP FAITH IN YOUR MATE'S LOVE FOR YOU EVEN WHEN FOR A
TIME HE OR SHE DOES NOT 102

\# 52 • SUCCESS DOESN'T DEPEND ON HOW MANY TIMES YOU FALL BUT
ON HOW MANY TIMES YOU GET BACK UP 104

\# 53 • TRIALS AND TRIBULATIONS ARE TO MAKE, NOT BREAK YOU 106

\# 54 • BE TRUE TO WHAT INSPIRES YOU 108

\# 55 • LOVE IS BEST WITHOUT STRINGS ATTACHED; NO "IFS" OR "BUTS" 110

\# 56 • DO WHAT YOU LOVE; LOVE WHAT YOU DO 112

\# 57 • FRIENDSHIP IS ESSENTIAL TO LOVE 114

\# 58 • YOU AND YOUR PARTNER MAY NOT BE ALIKE IN YOUR
TOLERANCE OR DESIRE FOR INTIMACY 116

\# 59 • A CRISIS IS AN OPPORTUNITY FOR LOVE TO GROW 118

\# 60 • CULTIVATE AN ATTITUDE OF GRATITUDE 120

\# 61 • CREATE A LOVE NEST 122

\# 62 • HEARTFELT MASSAGE 124

\# 63 • SLOW DOWN; SAVOR YOUR LOVER 126

\# 64 • PUT LOVE FIRST TO MAKE PASSION LAST 128

\# 65 • INTIMATE SEX TALKS 130

\# 66 • IF YOU'RE BORED, MAYBE YOU'VE LET YOURSELF BECOME BORING 132

\# 67 • YOUR SEXUAL FULFILLMENT IS PRIMARILY UP TO YOU, NOT YOUR
LOVE PARTNER 134

\# 68 • ENJOY X-RATED FANTASY 136

\# 69 • DIVINE SEX 138

\# 70 • MEDITATING OPENS THE HEART 140

\# 71 • SPIRITUAL VALUES 142

\# 72 • WHAT YOU DON'T GIVE, YOU LOSE 144

INDEX □ 149

NATASHA JOSEFOWITZ, PH.D., was born in Paris of Russian parents and is fluent in three languages. She earned her master's degree at forty and her doctorate at fifty. She is an adjunct professor at the School of Social Work at San Diego State University and a columnist, writing weekly on management issues. Dr. Josefowitz is a bestselling author and an award-winning poet. She has written three books on management: *Paths to Power: A Woman's Guide From First Job to Top Executive, You're the Boss: A Guide to Managing People With Understanding and Effectiveness,* and *Fitting In: How to Get a Good Start in Your New Job,* as well as five books of humorous verse and a book for children called *A Hundred Scoops of Ice Cream.* Her books have been translated into more than a dozen languages.

Dr. Josefowitz is an internationally known keynote speaker and has had her own television segment for eight years and a weekly program on public radio. She has been a guest on such programs as the *Dr. Ruth Show* and *Larry King Live.* Her articles have been published in *Harvard Business Review, Psychology Today, Ms.* magazine, *Business Horizons, Reader's Digest,* The *Washington Post, The New York Times, Los Angeles Times,* and the London *Times.* She has been named Woman of the Year by the Los Angeles Women in Management Association and has received the Living Legacy Award from the Women's International Center. Natasha is also the mother and stepmother of five children, has seven grandchildren, and lives in La Jolla, California.

HAROLD H. BLOOMFIELD, M.D., is one of the leading psychological educators of our time. An eminent Yale-trained psychiatrist, Dr. Bloomfield introduced meditation, holistic health, and family peacemaking to millions of people. He is an adjunct professor of psychology at Union Graduate School.

Dr. Bloomfield is the coauthor of the recent bestseller, the revised edition of *How to Survive the Loss of a Love*. His book, *TM*, was on the *New York Times* bestseller list for over six months and he is the author or coauthor of other bestsellers, such as *Making Peace With Your Parents*, *Making Peace With Yourself*, *Inner Joy*, *Lifemates*, and *Making Peace in Your Stepfamily*. His books have sold more than five million copies and have been translated into twenty-two languages.

Dr. Bloomfield is among the world's most sought-after keynote speakers and seminar leaders for public appearances, educational programs, and conferences. He is a frequent guest on *Oprah Winfrey*, *Donahue*, *Sally Jessy Raphael*, *Larry King Live*, CNN, and *ABC News*. In addition to professional journals, his work and popular articles appear in *USA Today*, *Los Angeles Times*, *San Francisco Examiner*, *Cosmopolitan*, *Ladies' Home Journal*, *New Woman*, and *American Health*.

Dr. Bloomfield is the recipient of the Medical Self-Care Magazine Book of the Year Award, the Golden Apple Award for Outstanding Psychological Educator, and the American Holistic Health Association's Lifetime Achievement Award.

In addition to his writing and research work, Dr. Bloomfield maintains a private clinical practice and is director of psychiatry, psychotherapy, and family counseling at the North County Health Center in Del Mar, California. He is a member of the American Psychiatric Association and the San Diego Psychiatric Society. He lives with his wife, Sirah, and their three children in Del Mar, California.